THE SHURI EFFECT

THE SHURI EFFECT

BRIDGING THE GAP FOR YOUNG BLACK WOMEN IN STEM

LAURYN MWALE

NEW DEGREE PRESS

THE SHURI EFFECT

Bridging the Gap for Young Black Women in STEM

ISBN   978-1-63730-708-3 *Paperback*

978-1-63730-799-1 *Kindle Ebook*

979-8-88504-007-5 *Ebook*

To the dreamers and the bookworms

CONTENTS

INTERVIEWEE BIOS   11

INTRODUCTION   21

PART I.   **SETTING THE STAGE**   **27**

CHAPTER 1.   STARTING WITH WHY   29

CHAPTER 2.   BELIEVING YOU CAN   47

INTERLUDE: BLACK WOMEN ON

SELF-EFFICACY   61

INTERLUDE: THE WAY I SEE THE WORLD:

A STATEMENT OF POSITIONALITY   65

CHAPTER 3.   BUILDING THE WORLD FOR

THE DEFAULT WHITE MALE   69

CHAPTER 4.   AFRICAN WOMANHOOD   83

INTERLUDE: BLACK WOMEN ON

BENEVOLENT SEXISM   95

CHAPTER 5.   ACCESS GAPS   101

INTERLUDE: BLACK WOMEN ON ACCESS

AND SUPPORT SYSTEMS   115

PART II.   **ALLY IS A VERB AND**

SO IS RACIST   **119**

INTERLUDE: CAN THEY REALLY NOT SEE

ME? OR ARE THEY STARING?   121

CHAPTER 6.   AN INTRODUCTION TO THE

MICROAGGRESSION   125

INTERLUDE: BLACK WOMEN ON
MICROAGGRESSIONS 139
INTERLUDE: SOMETIMES PEOPLE SURPRISE
YOU 143
CHAPTER 7. A NOTE TO ALLIES 149
INTERLUDE: BLACK WOMEN TO ALLIES 155

PART III. **THE EARLY YEARS** **163**
INTERLUDE: DOCTOR, LAWYER, ENGINEER 165
CHAPTER 8. TEACHERS, ANXIETY
TRANSFER, AND STEREOTYPE
THREAT 169
INTERLUDE: BLACK WOMEN ON
STEREOTYPES AND
EXPECTATIONS 177
INTERLUDE: THE SHURI EFFECT: WHAT
SHURI MEANS TO ME 183
CHAPTER 9. THE SCULLY EFFECT AND THE
IMPACT OF ROLE MODELS IN
MEDIA 189
INTERLUDE: BLACK WOMEN ON ROLE
MODELS 197
CHAPTER 10. WHO IS A SCIENTIST? 203
CHAPTER 11. WHAT CAN WE DO FOR YOUNG
GIRLS? 207

PART IV. **TAKING UP SPACE IN FURTHER**
EDUCATION **213**
INTERLUDE: I REALLY SHOULDN'T BE HERE 215
CHAPTER 12. GETTING IN 219
CHAPTER 13. RACIST PLACES AND FACES 225
INTERLUDE: BLACK WOMEN ON UNIVERSITY 233

CHAPTER 14. WHAT CAN WE DO FOR BLACK
WOMEN IN HIGHER EDUCATION? 241

PART V.   **BLACK GIRL SURVIVAL GUIDE**   **247**
CHAPTER 15. IMPOSTER SYNDROME 101   249
CHAPTER 16. MANAGING YOUR MENTAL
HEALTH   257
CHAPTER 17. A PERSONAL MANIFESTO IN
TEN SUGGESTIONS   265
INTERLUDE: ADVICE FROM AND FOR BLACK
WOMEN   273

CONCLUSION   **279**
INTERLUDE: BLACK WOMEN ON BEING
INSPIRED AND THE MOMENTS
THEY FELL IN LOVE WITH STEM 287

ACKNOWLEDGMENTS   293
APPENDIX   297

INTERVIEWEE BIOS

This book is for and about Black women, and many people were generous enough to share their stories with me. You will find select quotes from our conversations sprinkled throughout the chapters and in their own dedicated sections. Thank you, ladies!

OYINDA ADENIYI

Oyinda is a medical student at the Hull York Medical School and a co-founder at Black Excellence Network. She is passionate about social enterprise. In recognition of the systemic challenges that Black students and students of underrepresented backgrounds face, she strives to widen participation and create positive change.

SADIQAH MUSA

Sadiqah is an experienced senior data analyst with a demonstrated history of working in the energy and publishing sectors. She is the co-founder of Black in Data, a collaborative movement for people of color, striving to promote equality of opportunity and representation within the data industry.

BLESSING ADOGAME

Blessing is an ardent creative who leverages the digital world. Blessing believes that behind every name lies context to a person's worldview, challenges, and ambitions—all of which influence their leadership, creativity, or innovation. As someone born in Nigeria who has lived in Germany, Scotland, and the United States before the age of eighteen, she has an atypical perspective and background, all of which she uses to her advantage and for the benefit of others.

HAJER KAROUI

Hajer grew up in Tunisia until the age of nineteen when she moved to the USA and obtained a bachelor of science in computer science with a minor in neuroscience. She worked in app development and cybersecurity, but her passion for brain sciences led her to pursue a master's of research in neuroscience at Imperial College London, where she currently works as a data manager and researcher.

DANIELLE GEATHERS

Danielle is a student at Massachusetts Institute of Technology where she studies mechanical engineering with a concentration in product design. In 2020, she became the first Black woman student body president of MIT in its 159-year history.

NTOMBIZODWA MAKUYANA

Ntombizodwa, or Tombi, is a PhD student at Babraham Institute University of Cambridge and a Gates Scholar researching respiratory immunology. Tombi graduated from the Barrett Honors College at Arizona State University (ASU) with a bachelor's degree in medicinal chemistry (biochemistry) with the Mastercard Foundation Program. Ntombi aspires to contribute to efforts of improving healthcare standards in Africa and promoting women empowerment.

ANGELA V. HARRIS

Angela is a high-impact, collaborative thought leader and philanthropist with over twenty years of business experience helping companies deliver technology solutions. She has a passion for causes supporting women and underrepresented students in the tech industry. Angela lives by Gandhi's famous words, "Be the change you wish to see in the world."

DR. SALOME MASWIME

Salome is an associate professor and the head of the global surgery division at the University of Cape Town; an obstetrician and gynecologist; a World Economic Forum Young Scientist; Next Einstein Fellow and president of the South African Clinician Scientists Society. She is a former research fellow at Massachusetts General Hospital and Harvard Medical School and former lecturer at the Wits University. She is a trustee of the South African Health Systems Trust, an associate editor of the South African Journal of Obstetrics and Gynaecology, and a member of UNITARs' Global Surgery Foundation leadership team.

AMA OWUSU-AFRIYIE

Ama is the founder of NovaTuition, an organization that enables students to develop life-long skills and achieve their desired grades by offering affordable and accessible online one-to-one tuition and personal development training for students. She has a bachelor's degree in chemistry from the University of Nottingham.

DR. MALIKA GRAYSON

Malika is the founder of STEMinist Empowered LLC, an organization focused on the empowerment of Women of Color who pursue graduate degrees. Her work in STEM has led to her being named one of Trinidad and Tobago's 40 Under 40 Youth Influencers by the country's Ministry of Youth and Sports Affairs. She is also the author of the bestselling book *Hooded: A Black Girl's Guide to the PhD* and has been featured in a number of publications and books including *US Black Engineer and Information Technology* magazine and *Radiations* magazine.

ABADESI OSUNSADE

Abadesi is the founder and CEO of Hustle Crew, a company that helps tech teams optimize for inclusion in key decisions from hiring to product design. She is the co-host of the "Techish" podcast, a top-twenty tech podcast, and in 2016, she published her careers advice book, *Dream Big Hustle Hard: A Millennial Woman's Guide to Success in Tech*, which is rated five stars on Amazon. She has worked in various tech companies throughout her career.

TRACEY ABAYETA

Tracey is a relationship coach, founder of Opportunity Central, an initiative working to raise awareness of career opportunities among students from BAME backgrounds across the UK, and investment banker turned HR professional.

YVONNE BAJELA

Yvonne is a founding principal at Impact X Capital. In 2020, she was named one of the 25 Leading Black British Business People to Follow and made the Forbes 30 Under 30 list under the category of finance.

BUSOLA BANJO

Busola is a Nigerian-British chartered electrical engineer with an MBA from INSEAD Business School. She currently works as a manager at Siemens Energy.

DR. EMILY SENA

Dr. Emily Sena is a neuroscientist, meta-research scientist, and Stroke Association funded senior lecturer at the University of Edinburgh. She co-founded and was co-convenor of the university's Race Equality Network, and now convenes their Race Equality and Anti-Racist Sub-Committee and is highly committed to engendering and facilitating an anti-racist culture across campus.

ESTIFA'A ZAID

Estifa'a is an experimental particle physics PhD student at the University of Edinburgh.

BOLA AJOSE

Bola is a self-taught programmer and passionate about STEM communication and amplifying Black women's voices within this space. She works as a technical operations analyst at the data platform Permutive, with previous experience as a logistics manager for Stemettes, and program manager at Coders of Colour.

TUMI AKEKE

Tumi is a final-year biochemistry student and a MasterCard Foundation Scholar at the University of Edinburgh. Based on her passion for gender, racial, and health equality, she founded two social enterprises, Oncoreality and The BlackED Movement. Her interests are cancer medicine, reading, traveling, and dancing.

ALDA MANUEL

Alda is an Angolan renewable energy project manager, electrical engineer, ambassador for the Next Einstein Forum, and advocate for women and girls.

ASHLEY LINDALÍA WALKER

Ashley is an astrochemist, science communicator, and activist. In response to police brutality against Black Americans and sparked by the success of Black Birders Week, Walker co-organized #BlackinChem, #BlackInAstro, and #BlackInPhysics to highlight and amplify the voices of Black researchers and scholars in these fields.

OYINDAMOLA OYEWUMI

Oyindamola is an early-years educator and a curriculum developer. She advocates for early childhood literacy, inclusion, child protection, and upholding teaching as a professional career.

AISHA THOMAS

A born and bred Bristolian, Aisha studied law at the University of the West of England before transitioning to education in 2010. In 2016, Aisha became assistant principal at an inner-city secondary school in Bristol. Specializing in equality, diversity, inclusion, and belonging (EDIB), she's a passionate educational activist with a particular interest in race and anti-racist practice. Since then, Aisha has advocated for equitable representation in education and the wider world. Her work has included presenting a BBC documentary about the lack of Black teachers in Bristol, delivering a 2019 TEDx Bristol talk "Why Representation Really Matters," and, in 2020, launching her organization, Representation Matters Ltd.

CECIRAHIM SESAY

Cecirahim is a current master of public health in epidemiology and biostatistics student at the Dornsife School of Public Health at Drexel University. In 2020, she started The Plain, an organization focused on combating misinformation surrounding public health issues.

SINÉAD OBENG

Sinéad is a regulatory affairs advisor and the vice-chair of the Young Professionals network of the Energy Institute.

MBALI HLONGWANE

Mbali's personal vision is to drive the economic and social development of Africa at large by upskilling and positioning women to participate in the tech transformation. Mbali believes Africa cannot innovate and advance without getting women involved. Due to the existing gap within the tech sector, Mbali wants to use technology, knowledge sharing, integrity, and sustainable business models to ensure that one million women in Africa receive the tech skills needed to build solutions, start companies, and take up executive roles in tech organizations—all by 2030.

DR. RHONDA VONSHAY SHARPE

Rhonda is an American economist who is the founder and current president of the Women's Institute for Science, Equity, and Race (WISER), the first think tank to focus solely on the social, economic, cultural, and political well-being of women of color. She is a feminist economist who has been a faculty member at an extensive list of colleges and universities and served as president of the National Economic Association from 2017 to 2018.

KARRIN MAYFIELD FELTON

Karrin is a self-professed geek with over twenty years of engineering experience and leadership in the private and public sectors. She is a STEM advocate, mentor, dynamic speaker, and thought leader who pursues intentional outreach that prepares students and early career professionals to succeed while facing emerging challenges.

JASMINE MACK

Jasmine is an NIH Oxford-Cambridge Scholar completing doctoral training between the National Institute of Environmental Health Sciences and the University of Cambridge. She earned her bachelor of science from Emory University, master of public health from Boston University, and master of science in biostatistics from the University of Michigan.

REGINA MTONGA

Regina is the co-founder and director at Asikana Network, an organization in Zambia that seeks to increase the number of women and girls actively participating in technology in Zambia. She is the assistant director of Zambian Feminist and an award recipient of the Queen's Young Leaders Programme.

DR. OLAMIDE DADA

Olamide is the founder and chief executive of Melanin Medics, a charity that supports present and future African and Caribbean doctors. Olamide is also passionate about ethnic health inequalities, social entrepreneurship, and empowering young people. She is an alumnus of the Healthcare Leadership Academy and a Fellow of the Institute of Leadership and Management. She also sits on the equality and diversity advisory board in the General Medical Council and in the British Medical Association. Olamide has been the recipient of multiple awards including the We Are the City Rising Star in Healthcare 2020 award.

INTRODUCTION

It was the first day of the semester.

I felt good about this one. I am one of those "new year, new me" people who sees January as an opportunity to level up. I am also not a morning person. These two things exist in a precarious suspension. I woke up early enough to make it, but slightly too late to stroll to my destination. Once dressed, I grabbed my bag and made my way down the buzzing streets and the seemingly never-ending incline to Kings Buildings, the science campus of the University of Edinburgh. I had checked my calendar the week before and remembered the lecture theater I needed to get to. I walked in right as the lecturer began speaking and quickly sat in the third row to avoid drawing too much attention to myself.

Now, I immediately knew I was in the wrong lecture theater. When I walked through the door, I saw three other Black people.

Three!

Not Nia or Ben, the other two Black girls in a few of my classes, but three strange faces. I looked at the blackboard in front of me, but as the lecturer had yet to begin teaching, it held no clues. It was the second half of my third year. These people simply could not have jumped out of nowhere. "What was going on?" I thought as shame descended on me, a niggling feeling that I had foolishly walked into the wrong crowded lecture on the first day and now had to draw even more attention to myself by walking out. Finally, the projector lit up.

I was definitely not in my honors algebra course. I knew I was in the wrong place because too many people looked like me.

———

My experience throughout my undergraduate studies is as the only or—sometimes when I'm lucky—one of two or three Black students in my courses. I am the only Black female mathematician in my graduating class, a graduating class that has nearly two hundred students and is nearly 50 percent female.

My experience is not unique. One US estimate states that only 2.9 percent of STEM degrees are awarded to Black women (National Center for Education Statistics, 2018). *Two-point-nine percent.* Being a Black woman in STEM is an integral part of my persona now. Studying at a predominantly white institution obviously means it's a very white space. Once you include the STEM aspect, people who look like me are unicorns. The brilliant scientist or great innovator caricature is very white, very male, and honestly, doesn't seem like a fun person to be around.

Before *Hidden Figures*, I had no one to look to. I did have Ada Lovelace and Rosalind Franklin, brilliant women whose work fundamentally changed the world we live in, but sexism and racism are very distinct biases that create different lived experiences. I desperately needed a more representative role model and the magic that is *Hidden Figures*, the strength of its performances, and most importantly, the unveiling of the stories of Katherine Johnson, Mary Jackson, and Dorothy Vaughan, changed my life. Here were Black female mathematicians. That film legitimized my choices and identity. Then, I saw *Black Panther* and fell in love with Shuri. She was snarky and brilliant and seeing her made me realize how starved I was for fictional Black STEM brilliance.

As a society, we believe we have made a massive amount of progress. And, in many ways, we have. Worldwide, more girls, of all backgrounds, are in school for longer. Governments are placing more focus on gender equality and education. Enrollment in further education is generally trending upward, and more women are receiving undergraduate degrees than men. All of this is commendable.

Now, let's texturize the picture. Globally, women account for less than a third of scientific research and development employees (UNESCO Institute for Statistics [2019]). One hundred and nineteen countries have never had a female head of state, and of the women who do become

ministers, the top five commonly held responsibilities
are (Inter-Parliamentary Union and UN Women [2020]):

1. Family, children, youth, the elderly, and/or the
   disabled
2. Social affairs
3. Environment, natural resources, and/or energy
4. Employment, labor, and/or vocational training
5. Women's affairs and/or gender equality

In the United Kingdom, female graduates from core STEM
subjects made up 25 percent of the total in 2015 and 26
percent of the total in 2019. We can fairly assume that
this ratio gets worse when you consider Black women.
One in ten African girls misses school time because of
their period (Actionaid) and of the thirty-one million
girls currently out of primary education, seventeen million are not expected to enter education at any time in
their lives (Education for all Global Monitoring Report,
2013). This is not progress.

I decided to write this book because I need to understand
what's going on. I was discouraged from pursuing my
undergraduate degree in maths for a lot of reasons by
a lot of people. I almost believed them. Maybe I wasn't
smart enough. Maybe it would be hard and boring—a
lot of maybes. And, in hindsight, they were all wrong.
It has been challenging, on occasion, extremely difficult
and massively fulfilling. On a lot of days, I have felt out
of place and out of my depth, an admissions error and
an eyesore. Fortunately, I'm stubborn, and I stuck with

it. Despite it being incredibly tough and hearing a lot of dumb comments, I have had an amazing time.

As I write this chapter, I'm completing the final semester of my undergraduate degree online due to the coronavirus pandemic. I have done an incredible amount of research and encountered so many powerhouse role models. However, there are still not enough Black women in STEM. Why? I simply cannot imagine a good enough reason. I am a reasonably confident person, so take this statement at face value; I am not especially brilliant or special. All I had was an interest supported by a few good teachers and a support system when it got hard. Admittedly, I was also really lucky. I had taken the right subjects, had access to good quality educational facilities, had good enough grades, and had the funding to choose something out of interest and not economic necessity.

How can we create that cocktail of accessibility for other Black women? That's a question I pose to educators, advocates, policy makers, parents, young Black women like myself, allies, and anyone curious enough to pick up this book.

In this book, I attempt to unpack all of the reasons why there are not more Black women in STEM. This is because it's an issue close to my heart and one of many inexplicable modern status quos that need to be changed now. I'm writing it for young women like me who are also asking themselves why, for allies and advocates, and for anyone who wants to understand why the problem exists and wants to know how it could be improved. We will explore topics such as intersectionality, self-efficacy, and microaggressions. I will introduce you to some Black women you need to know and celebrate as well as include excerpts from interviews with incredible role models of mine who speak from their own experiences and expertise. To breathe life into the statistics and research, I will share some personal stories, both happy and infuriating from my own journey. What I am attempting to do is write the very book I needed four years ago.

This book is, in part, about all the blockades and some ways we can fix them. These structural barriers need to be dismantled so everyone can pursue every kind of dream, regardless of who they are, especially if they are currently underrepresented. This book is about being whomever you want, doing whatever you want with the fairest chances. If you want to be a civil engineer, a chemist, or a video game designer, I hope this book is interesting, empowering, and useful. However, if you want to be a classical pianist, an English teacher, or an economist, do that. Our diversity of thoughts, interests, and ideas is what makes the world inspiring. Regardless of who you are and what you do, know that I'm cheering you on.

PART 1

SETTING THE STAGE

CHAPTER 1

STARTING WITH WHY

The only thing separating women of color from anyone else is opportunity.

—VIOLA DAVIS

I remember the moment perfectly.

It was the first official meeting of my future graduating class on campus. My phone was dead, but I had scanned a map before I left my halls of residence and hoped for the best. Luckily, I noticed a red-haired girl walking ahead of me moving in the same general direction, looking just as lost as I was. At an intersection, I asked her where she was going, and she mentioned the same building. I introduced myself, and we decided to wander over together. In transit, we collected four more lost souls. Maybe forty minutes later, we walked into the building, received our welcome packets, and began the awkward networking. Laughing across the room, I saw a girl with glittery clips in her hair and realized we were the only Black people there.

The chatter around me faded to a hum and I suddenly felt very cold. My eyes frantically scanned the room once, twice, three times before I allowed it to dawn on me. We were unicorns. Someone asked me a question and pulled me out of my spiral. I smiled and rejoined the experience. That night, I scoured Google for data and came across a statistic from the American National Centre for Education Statistics. Let me remind you: Two-point-nine percent of STEM graduates are Black women. Of course, in the African context, this statistic would be a lot less bleak. That doesn't mean a problem does not exist. Only 30 percent of researchers in Sub-Saharan Africa are women (World Health Organisation, 2015).

Like all social questions, this one is multifaceted and incredibly complex.

THE LEAKY PIPELINE

The leaky pipeline is a metaphor used to explain how women become a minority in STEM. It is overly simplistic and, in many ways, inappropriate, but let's begin our exploration here. We assume infinite possibilities for every child. Newborn babies are pretty interchangeable. The differences come in later and are prompted by conditioning, access, individual grit, and available support. But, right at the beginning, despite the proclamations of their parents, newborns aren't yet remarkable, especially talented, or specifically skilled. They truly have boundless options. They can become politicians, music megastars, and, given the topic of this book, excel in all manner of STEM-related pursuits.

Imagine that the water flowing through a pipeline represents Black and self-identifying female individuals at various levels in STEM education, careers, and engagement. For argument's sake, we assume that all little Black girls enter the pipeline at the beginning, regardless of background. And as we move along, they begin to "leak out." For example, this happens when students transition to secondary school or high school and are allowed to choose their own subjects. Access to adequate educational facilities, imposed stereotypes and ambitions, as well as the absence of role models, are some reasons why young women are less likely to opt into STEM education. Thus, they have leaked out of the pipeline. Another mass exodus occurs upon the completion of an advanced qualification. Maybe she has been warned of the hostility of academia or male-dominated professional environments toward qualified women. In which case, she may rationally decide to opt into a space that is more supportive of her needs as a mother or with higher odds of her being listened to and promoted. As Salome stated,

We need to create the right environment for Black women. We can study, get the degrees and qualifications but when we move into the (professional) space, it can be very hostile toward us; we are not being promoted or taken seriously. You literally need to fight your way up to the top and a lot of women give up on their way there. I think there's a lot that can be done just to allow Black women to feel like it's their space as well. And there are a lot of competing interests, for us, as African women, you've got your family to look after and many other activities. Some people may want to go down the academic route but begin to realize their time and energy will be better spent elsewhere, and they'll make a career change. How do we retain the talent that we've got?

The leaky pipeline metaphor is used because it is easy to visualize and understand. However, it is too simplistic for the following reasons.

- This pipeline inherently implies that all participants flowing through it are homogenous. That's simply absurd. Structural factors like class and institutionalized sexism and racism will stall or even halt the progress of Black women through the pipeline.
- The pipeline implies the end goal should be an advanced STEM degree, and anything besides that is a leak or failure. This is also ridiculous because a lot of value is in participating in STEM education to a certain extent for a specific reason. This could be studying biology to work in science policy or studying maths to become a teacher. These are valuable occupations and destinations. Besides this, science engagement for fun is another destination we should acknowledge, legitimize, and celebrate.
- This model does not allow people to flow back in. There is a wealth of resources available online that empowers people to self-teach. Coding, for example, can be honed without engaging with an academic institution and utilized to enter the STEM workforce.
- Education is sadly not as accessible as this pipeline implies. We don't opt out. We are more accurately pushed out, and that is the issue at hand. Not performative inclusion and diversity, but egalitarian

access to education and support when pursuing opportunities.

You didn't make good choices. You had good choices. Options that being rich, and white, and entitled gave you.

—MIA WARREN, *LITTLE FIRES EVERYWHERE*

BARRIERS AFFECTING BLACK WOMEN

Circumstantial factors and systemic barriers prevent or make it significantly difficult to become a Black woman in STEM. The following list of reasons is far from exhaustive.

STRICT REQUIREMENTS AND EXPECTATIONS

Some STEM programs may focus more on rigid, sequential thought processes at the expense of more holistic thinking approaches. At the risk of leaning too heavily into stereotypes, I will say research has shown women to be strong critical thinkers who use multiple lenses and perspectives to scrutinize an issue. If such thinking isn't welcomed or celebrated, they may think they don't have the innate ability to engage. Additionally, science tends to be hierarchical; one often needs to have certain prerequisites to engage at the next level. This disadvantages people in a multitude of ways. Many people lack the economic and/or social capital to have gone from general education to university while making the "right" academic choices and assembling the "right" extracurriculars. A history of positive engagement serves you and class, gender, locality, and other social factors may compromise or prevent you from building this history. Returning to a STEM pathway later has high opportunity, time, and financial costs.

There was no STEM education. Prior to college, I taught myself basic programming, which was nowhere on the level of C++. So, I struggled during my freshman year, trying to learn and understand the content. When I was looking at my course to study for the next three, four years of school, it didn't seem appealing to me to remain a computer science major.

—ANGELA

ISOLATION

We hear a lot about the male-dominance in STEM fields. Being the sole female will aggravate and intensify imposter syndrome. You may experience tokenism, the result of performative recruitment actions. Pastoral support may be unavailable or insufficient to provide the kind of support required to aid Black and female students or professionals.

So for Black women, you might wonder, "Okay, am I really here because of my skill, because of my expertise, or am I just here because I'm another Black face, you know, to put on posters and things like that?"

—BLESSING

THE CULTURE

We have a shared cultural understanding of who is an innovator. It is male, often antisocial with the audacity to believe that they can change the world. This stereotype paints women with otherhood and makes it more difficult to gain admission into STEM spaces and be adequately included once they are present. In her book, *Brotopia*, Emily Chang describes the legacy of stereotype as hiring criteria in Silicon Valley. Concerning examples include Christa Quarles—the current CEO of the online restaurant booking service Open Table—being taken to a strip club during a job interview to see if she could fit in, and Janica Alverez—the CEO of breast pump company, Naya—being questioned by investors of her commitment to the company as a mother, while her husband and business partner didn't receive the same scrutiny.

I remember an incident with a former boss. One Friday afternoon, he showed up at my desk. And he said, "Listen, all the women who are in computer science are either wacky looking or have face tattoos and you're neither of those. So, I don't know, maybe go and get a degree in business or something." This was during my sophomore year. I decided to ignore it, sweep it under the rug. I was scared of losing my power and of him treating me more harshly. I wish someone had reached out to me. Someone who was an HR official who cared about the minority women on professional placements and could protect me.

—HAJER

WORK-LIFE BALANCE ISSUES

Women do an incredible amount of unpaid labor. Activities such as cooking, cleaning, and the mental load of home management are estimated to contribute £140 billion to the economy of the United Kingdom (Anderson, 2020) and $1.5 trillion to the US economy (Ghodsee and Wezerek, 2020). Little attempt has been made to approximate the contribution of women's unpaid labor in the African context which very clearly shows how much value is ascribed to it. McKinsey estimates that gender equality will add twelve trillion dollars to the global economy (McKinsey, 2020). STEM students and professionals often speak of a culture of overwork; the expectation that everyone will cope with complicated projects involving high time commitment over relatively short timescales. For someone who is the main caregiver to an elderly parent or a small child, a position women often occupy, it can be an impossible balancing act.

When you consider the plight of young girls, the unpaid labor gap continues. Girls between five and fourteen spend 160 million more hours on household chores than boys of the same age (UNICEF, 2016). This cultural expectation that girls should be training for marriage and motherhood robs them of time that could be used to study, participate in enrichment activities, or simply have fun. In extreme cases, this means that girls are pulled out of school to support the family, in deference to their brothers who must finish school as future breadwinners.

As a scientist, we do all sorts of things that take us out of the home. You need support; a family that believes in you and is able to pitch in when you have to travel and leave the kids; having a husband that tells you to go for it and mentors who see your talent, open opportunities and create networks for you to excel.

—SALOME

NON-EXISTENT AND INEFFECTIVE SOCIAL NETWORKS

Networks of supporters and advisors are necessary features to surviving and thriving in any environment. Being the token girl or token minority or both deprives you of a natural network of people who look like you, which could cause you to exit the pipeline because you feel unsupported and unwelcome. The availability and effectiveness of formal mentorship programs for Black women at the beginning of their careers is hampered by the lack of representation at higher rungs; the critical mass hasn't been reached. People are complex and multifaceted. Having a mentor who looks like you, has experienced things that you might, and can provide authentic, lived-in advice, is not a given for Black women in STEM.

When I went in, I didn't have people of color around me. I was really surrounded by a sea of white, and it also included people from really privileged backgrounds. There was a complete lack of understanding of who people of color were and what they went through. My first year was dominated by having to constantly explain my experience to people. And it was different layers of that experience because people didn't really understand how my identities intersected. They didn't understand how I could be Muslim and a woman, or Muslim and Black. And you don't really understand what they take issue with, because it could be one of the three or all of them so that first year was a steep learning curve. It was fun. It was probably one of the best years of my life. Though in hindsight, it was tough.

—ESTIFA'A

GOOD OLD CLASSISM

Due to historical legacies such as Jim Crow in America and the long-term impact of colonialism in Africa, Black people, especially Black women, are often in spaces with poorer schools and public libraries, little to no access to digital devices with a strong internet connection, and so on. This makes it that much harder for them to engage with STEM, study the content effectively, and get the grades that would allow it to be a long-term career option.

I wish more professors took time to actually learn about their students' experiences and backgrounds to be better educators. For example, it's knowing that some people don't have access to certain classes in high school. We find that many Black people don't have access to advanced classes, right? So then when you teach a computer science class, you can't start from a place of assuming that everyone has taken an AP Computer Science class. These things won't necessarily come to your mind until you have met, perhaps, like one to five Black students who have said, "Yeah, I didn't take this class in high school. So, I'm coming here with no knowledge." It's a matter of just listening

to students and listening so that you can take the stories you're
hearing and implement them in your teaching style.

—ANGELA

GOOD OLD MISOGYNY

You expected this one, didn't you? Misogyny is the hatred of, contempt for, or prejudice against women or girls. It propagates sexism by enforcing an inferior status on women. It manifests as exclusion, discrimination, patriarchy, belittling, disenfranchisement, and violence against women, among other things. Misogyny exists to stop the advancement of women.

I got so used to comments from teachers. Whenever I beat my male classmates, the teacher would say, "Can you imagine a girl got the highest marks? How can you let her beat you as a boy?" and this comment wouldn't be made if a boy got the highest grade. I also remember that when they picked teams for competitions, even though girls and boys may be equally smart, it would be a team dominated by the boys.

—TUMI

GOOD OLD RACISM

The oxymoron that is *"separate but equal"*. The reality of racial discrimination, be it legally sanctioned or socially cultivated, transmits into resource allocation, the workload placed on teachers, class sizes, quality of lab equipment, access to up-to-date textbooks, and so on. Research has shown that Black students who are 18 percent of all US pre-schoolers make up almost 50 percent of pre-school suspensions (Ben & Jerry's). Yes, it starts as early as pre-school! That is how early racism taints the educational experience. And this presumption of guilt and pattern of harsher punishment continues throughout education and into the real world. Repeated suspensions and other factors lead more Black students to drop out.

When I was a freshman one person said something that really struck me. He said, "you're not going to help with the experiment, because you're dumb." So, I asked why. And then he said, "You're stupid because you come from Africa." I stood up for myself. I told him that what he said wasn't right. I didn't yell. I gave him the facts. I told him to email the professor and ask for my grades.

—TOMBI

MISOGYNOIR

This term was coined by Moya Bailey, a gay African American feminist who defined it "to describe the particular brand of hatred directed at black women...." This is where the experiences of Black girls in STEM most cleanly fit. You are both a dumb girl and an illiterate Black. You are more likely to come from an underfunded school district because of your race and because of your gender, you are more likely to have been specifically reminded that you are not a "science person." Besides this, you carry a specific racialized and gendered burden as you move through the world. Speaking about the possible dilution of the term, Ms. Bailey had this to say:

> *I was looking for precise language to describe why Renisha McBride would be shot in the face, or why the Onion would think it's okay to talk about Quvenzhané the way they did, or the hypervisibility of Black women on reality TV, the arrest of Shanesha Taylor, the incarceration of CeCe, Laverne and Lupita being left off the TIME list, the continued legal actions against Marissa Alexander, the Twitter dragging of Black women with hateful hashtags and supposedly funny Instagram images as well as how Black women are talked about in music. All these things bring to mind misogynoir and not general misogyny directed at women of color more broadly.*

For the systemic reasons described above, and those not mentioned, and the personal factors affecting individuals, we do not have enough Black women in STEM.

SOME POOR EXCUSES

How does one solve a problem? Acknowledging a problem is the first step. Next, we identify the root causes and evaluate current structures for their deficiencies; an attempt to answer the question, why does this problem exist? Thirdly, we propose interventions based on our understanding of the problem and its causes. Finally, we have to follow through with the interventions and evaluate their impact—a four-step theory of change. Seems easy enough, right? Sadly, we have a gap at the taking responsibility part. Policy makers, political thinkers, and random people on the internet love to share their takes on why racial and gender attainment gaps exist. I'm going to share a few of these here and explore why they are at best imperfect, at worst, purely idiotic.

THE MYTH OF MERITOCRACY

Meritocracy implies that people succeed purely based on their own merits. It is the idea that if you work hard enough, you will succeed. It is the bat often used by privileged people to beat the underprivileged with; it says you are not successful because you are lazy, underqualified, and undeserving, and these things are purely in your own control.

Meritocracy is a myth. Michael Kinsley, an American political commentator, said, "Inequalities of income, wealth, status are inevitable, and in a capitalist system even necessary."

I am not writing about the merits and negative consequences of capitalism but given that most people currently live in capitalist societies, let's explore this further. Capitalism claims to reward people for their hard work, and this implies that your effort is directly related to your results.

This idea ignores the reality that we all have different starting points. Two students putting in the same number of study hours may have completely different outcomes if one went to an elite private school while another went to an under-resourced public school. Beyond this, we must consider the historical legacies of inequality. In the United Kingdom, the eight highest-ranked schools sent as many pupils to Oxford and Cambridge, two of the world's highest-ranked universities, as three-quarters of all other schools (Sutton Trust, 2018). Let's entertain the obvious; students at these top eight schools are neither the smartest nor are they the hardest working students in the country. Obviously, they work hard but the reason why they get into such prestigious universities probably has more to do with the small class sizes, well-resourced libraries, and the support of highly qualified and hopefully comparatively better-paid teachers, their parents' ability to afford private tutors, and access to up-to-date and engaging learning material. They have everything pointing them in the direction of success.

On the other hand, it was found that at ages eleven and sixteen, the attainment gap was widest for students who came from disadvantaged backgrounds and those who were eligible for free school meals (Education Endowment Fund, 2017). Studies have found these characteristics are linked to one's odds of reaching the expected standard in reading, writing, and mathematics, which in turn impacts your odds of graduating.

So, it isn't that Black women aren't trying hard enough. Given meritocracy is a mere fantasy, their efforts, herculean, and persistent, aren't the only factor contributing to their odds of success.

THE IDEA OF RACIAL DIFFERENCES IN INTELLIGENCE

I refuse to entertain this idea with an argument. Any argument about someone's educational abilities that hinges on their racial identity is racist. Hence, it is inherently stupid and invalid. Thank you for coming to my TED Talk.

THE IDEA OF A GENDERED BRAIN

A girl cannot spend more than four, or, in occasional instances, five hours of force daily upon her studies, and leave sufficient margin for the general physical growth that she must make in common with a boy, and so for constructing a reproductive apparatus. If she puts as much force into her brain education as a boy, the brain or special apparatus will suffer.

—EDWARD CLARKE

Edward Clarke, a Harvard Medical professor, argued that education was dangerous for girls and women because the intellectual labor involved sent energy rushing from the ovaries to the brain and would negatively impact reproduction. He did not say the same about men. Ruben and Raquel Gur, University of Pennsylvania professors of psychiatry, neurology, and radiology, claimed "the greater facility of women with inter-hemispheric communications may attract them to disciplines that require integration rather than detailed scrutiny of narrowly characterised processes" as reasoning for the underrepresentation of women in Science (Ceci and Williams, 2007).

In 1873, Clarke wrote about the idea of a "female brain," an idea which was echoed in 2007 by the Gurs. The idea of a "female brain" greatly concerns me. As a concept, it is often used to support the opinion that women are simply unable to do certain "difficult" things. As a result of scientific inquiry, we need to critically engage with the construction and fallacies of studies. Women are under-represented in research samples, and the construction of a study can coerce its results. This is a larger concern and a global issue, which prompts me to critically question findings such as these.

In her article, "Will Working Mothers' Brains Explode? The Popular New Genre of Neurosexism," Cordelia Fine coined the term neurosexism to be "the bias in neuroscience of sex differences toward reinforcing harmful gender stereotypes." Antiquated ideas of what women can and cannot do gain legitimacy when they are echoed within neuroscience, regardless of their occasionally laughable scientific robustness. The idea that women feel and men think is mirrored through Simon Baron-Cohen's empathizing-systematizing (E-S) theory and supported by the fact that girls play with dolls and boys play with cars. In these studies, very little is done to engage with the fact that boys will be bought cars and girls will be bought dolls. I don't doubt the results of these studies show different-looking brains. However, their willingness to claim a binary reality that aligns with gender roles is a cause for concern.

As a concept, the gendered brain is entrenched in misogyny. I prefer to critically engage with the concept of neuroplasticity, the ability of neural networks in the brain to change through growth and reorganization. Our social scripts give men a lifetime of experiences with computers and LEGO toys, which results in a synthetic advantage and a differently connected brain. The same scripts provide women with a synthetic advantage with language and mediation, but these skills are not held in the same regard. Our experiences, more than our gender, affect our brains. Early exposure to books or computers will have a long-term impact on your affinity for and ability with these things.

WHERE TO GO FROM HERE?

From the structural and societal barriers to junk science, we are not left with a concrete or satisfying answer to the central question: why is a specific demographic of people systemically excluded from participating in innovation and knowledge production? What does this mean for health care and technology, role modeling, and representation? There are a lot of reasons one could give, and I will detail many of these in the upcoming chapters, but there is also the fundamental notion of fairness. It is not fair that Black women and girls are underrepresented in STEM and elsewhere. They have points of view and great ideas, and they deserve the right to explore, make mistakes, and create. They deserve to do this without suffering suspicion, disrespect, or undermining behaviors. They deserve to be able to come into their own peacefully and boldly.

CHAPTER 2

BELIEVING YOU CAN

"If any female feels she needs anything beyond herself to legit-imate and validate her existence, she is already giving away her power to be self-defining, her agency."

—bell hooks

I love my mom. She is one of my favorite people, and we do a fair amount of talking on the phone. She hated the distance between us when I left for university. She would badger me to no end with texts and phone calls, not accounting for our time difference. When I would finally call her back, she would sardonically say, "Glad you're alive" and feign busyness. She is the true source of my sarcasm. When something good happens, I tell her. And even though she doesn't understand what it is and why I'm so excited, she validates me, and I need that. When I'm struggling, I call her and bemoan the impossible task I am contending with. Even if she doesn't understand the stakes, she tells me that I can do it.

Now, my mom has this near-obscene confidence in her kids' abilities. My ten-year-old brother expressed an interest in cooking, and she has a Gordon Ramsey-sized future planned out for him. She can also be one of those stubborn people who pays no heed to practical and legitimate blockades. "Fix your mindset. If you believe you can do it, you can, and if you believe you can't, don't even try," she says in a sing-song voice. Is it patronizing? Definitely. Is she right? Probably. The more I have allowed myself to be courageous, the more has become possible. My energy and resilience grow in line with my self-belief. When it wavers, I recite the following Maya Angelou quote.

"Your crown has been bought and paid for. Put it on your head and wear it"

—MAYA ANGELOU

It means different things on different days. Most days, it reminds me that I am able. It is my birthright to be confident in my abilities. This feeling speaks to my self-perception, or more accurately, my self-efficacy.

SELF-EFFICACY

Self-efficacy is defined as your personal judgment of how well you can execute a plan of action in prospective situations (Bandura, 1977). It manifests in your ambitions and how proactive you are in achieving them. Anyone who is repeatedly told they can or cannot do something could create a reality that matches these beliefs. Inspiration calendars are filled with quotes about this: "whether you believe you can or you believe you can't, you're right," "the first step in achieving your dreams is believing in them," and, a personal favorite, "the people who are crazy enough to think they can change the world are the ones who do." Why would someone pursue something that they know in their heart and mind, they will fail at? Would you? I wouldn't. What about something you know you would be amazing at? Why wouldn't you pursue that? Your belief in yourself is one of the most influential factors in your pursuits: personal, academic, professional, or otherwise. It is a massive factor in your thoughts, plans, and perceptions of control over a situation.

Anecdotally, we as a society tend to perceive STEM subjects as *difficult*. Many people have had negative experiences in school or have seen a movie about a genius, which highlighted the complexities of their work. This impacts our own self-efficacy in relation to STEM and how we feed into the self-efficacy beliefs of others. This book will go into situations and concepts that frame the STEM experiences of Black women and girls, so an understanding of self-efficacy, what it means for ambitions and actions, and how it's built or reduced is a good place to start.

HIGHS AND LOWS

Self-efficacy can be both high and low or a confusing mixture of both. Having high self-efficacy implies a strong belief in your ability to successfully complete a task, win a contest, understand a concept, perform for an audience, secure a date with someone you find attractive, and the list goes on. On the other hand, having low self-efficacy implies a strong belief in your ability to fail at something, and these are the tasks you never want to try. We have all had that one subject at school that seemed impossible, so we daydreamed during lessons and gave each homework problem about two seconds of thought before giving up, or a gym session in which we expended 60 percent of our energy on complaining. A mixed self-efficacy can occur when you place a ceiling on your abilities in a specific arena. For example, being a strong swimmer who refuses to swim in the ocean or a strong singer who refuses to perform in public. In these cases, you know you have a competency in something and derive pleasure from practicing it but do not want to share your talent with others and expose yourself to negative outcomes, feedback, or backlash.

EXAMPLES OF PEOPLE WITH HIGH SELF-EFFICACY:

- A student who isn't a strong physics student but believes that with effort they can do well on the exam.
- A new graduate moving into a high-status job who is nervous about the responsibility but believes they will be successful.
- Someone who can't play an instrument but is excited to learn and perform in a recital.

EXAMPLES OF PEOPLE WITH LOW SELF-EFFICACY:

- A student who thinks math is difficult and doesn't think it's worth trying.

- Someone who failed to learn how to swim when they were younger and so thinks that they'll never learn.
- Someone who chooses not to apply to jobs in a certain industry, despite meeting a majority, if not all, of the prerequisites because they think they won't make it to the interview phase.

Your levels of self-efficacy are also not permanent. Receiving a lot of negative feedback can reduce it and receiving praise can increase it. Improving your own skill level, building a sense of pride, or positive self-talk can all improve your self-efficacy levels while developing a sense of shame or practicing negative self-talk can reduce your self-efficacy in that arena of your life.

THOUGHTS AND ACTIONS

WHEN YOU THINK YOU CAN'T

Someone with low self-efficacy in a specific task has little belief in their abilities. Whatever it is, they genuinely believe it is out of their reach. This can be after a negative experience or even before an attempt is made. The following are examples of ways that negative self-efficacy can impact how you perceive a task.

- You think something is harder than it actually is.
- You aren't able to break the task up into more manageable tasks and engage with it in a very erratic way.
- Obstacles make you want to give up.
- Negative comments make you feel worse but positive comments don't necessarily make you feel better.

- Positive previous experiences are considered "dumb luck" while negative previous experiences are confirmations of your innate inability.

My mum's refrain of "If you think you can't, then you can't," knowingly or not, frames the greatest issue with having low self-efficacy. It stops you from engaging with whatever task it is and closes you off from a learning opportunity. In the face of a seemingly insurmountable task and in a bid to practice self-preservation, you quit before you start.

WHEN YOU THINK YOU CAN

Someone with high self-efficacy has a lot of confidence and belief in their own abilities. I would be remiss to ignore the fallacy of excessively high self-efficacy. These people might not make an effort because of notions of their own supreme innate talent and natural perfection. This is the difference between confidence and cockiness. Confident people have a healthy belief in their talents and continue to make an effort to develop them, while cocky people are self-important and don't see the need to make a sincere effort. The following are examples of how a healthy level of positive self-efficacy impacts how you perceive a task.

- You think tasks are manageable, even when they are initially difficult.
- You are able to take the broad view of a task and so plan for the best course of action.
- Obstacles make you try harder, not quit.

- You don't let negative feedback get you down for too long.
- Negative previous experiences or failures are attributed to external factors and thought of as learning opportunities while positive previous experiences build your confidence in your abilities.

FACTORS AFFECTING SELF-EFFICACY

Canadian American psychologist Albert Bandura, who defined the concept of self-efficacy in the 1960s, identified the following factors that affect self-efficacy:

- Experience or enactive attainment
  - A high level of mastery will increase your self-efficacy as successful previous experiences have a great impact. Inversely unsuccessful experiences will negatively impact self-efficacy, but people who have survived failure build a level of resilience, which protects their self-efficacy from the negative impacts of failure.
- Modeling or vicarious experience
  - Seeing someone else succeed improves your own perceptions of your probability of success in the same task. It's the well-known adage: "If they can do it, I can do it too." This is why role models are vital in opening the eyes of young people to the range of opportunities available to them.

If that person looks like me, then perhaps they can relate to me. And that factor is extremely important because there are hurdles and obstacles we experienced in the work environment that I may or may not need assistance with learning how to overcome. It's certainly helpful when I have someone I can relate to or that I perceive I can relate to, in the same environment because they look like me and they are where I desire to go.

—LATONYA

- Social persuasion
  - Direct encouragement or discouragement from another person. This is tempered by who offers the comment; the opinion of someone you respect will have a greater impact; however, the words of a stranger can have an impact as well. Also, discouragement is more effective in reducing self-efficacy than encouragement is at increasing self-efficacy.

It's not always about the money. It's about whether my family or my community is going to support me. And this gets into the self-efficacy beliefs of Black women. She asks, "Will I be rejected by my community if I go and do something different or outside of the norm of what's accepted, given the environment or circles I'm in?" You may ask yourself, "how will they see me, how will I see myself, and what can I believe about myself?

—LATONYA

- Physiological factors
  - Your response to a physiological sensation impacts your thoughts about a scenario. Experiencing butterflies in your stomach before a presentation can be seen in two ways. Someone with low self-efficacy would see their nerves as evidence

of their innate inability while someone with high self-efficacy will see it as a normal occurrence that happens when you're about to do a task you see as important.

SELF-EFFICACY AND ITS LINKS TO OTHER THINGS

RESILIENCE
Resilience is being able to bounce back from failure. If you have a high level of self-efficacy, you are more able to bounce back because you know that failure doesn't define your abilities.

CONFIDENCE
High self-efficacy and confidence are distinct but inter-linked. They can reinforce each other in a positive cycle; confident people believe in themselves, are more likely to succeed and so pursue more experiences to build their self-efficacy. High self-efficacy through belief in your ability to successfully execute plans can build your confidence.

MOTIVATION
Motivation is your desire to achieve something, and self-efficacy is your belief in your abilities to achieve something. Small and big successes increase your belief in your abilities and also increase your motivation to con-tinue pursuing new heights.

LOCUS OF CONTROL

Locus of control defines the degree to which you believe that external forces determine the outcome of events in your life. An external locus of control places the power of determination with external forces while an internal locus of control places the power of determination within the individual. People with high self-efficacy believe they play a role in their success while people with low self-efficacy place the blame outside of themselves. However, this is a weak relationship. You can have high self-efficacy and still believe there was an unfair testing strategy used. It is, however, an important relationship because it can be empowering, and improve your self-efficacy if you feel like your actions determine your success.

That would be really the premise of where the research goes, at least for me. It's that competence; it's an internal locus of control that is required. But then there's that external context feeding into your self-belief.

—LATONYA

What does this all mean in the context of this book?

I had a conversation with LaTonya Jackson, EdD. She studied the self-efficacy beliefs of Black women leaders in Fortune 500 companies. Quotes from our interview are dotted about this chapter. I asked her how she would describe self-efficacy for Black women specifically, and she had the following to say:

When I look at Black women and their self-efficacy, I define it as "a belief about one's own ability to attain leadership." When you think about that, it's about competence and confidence. Well, it depends on your community, right? Because of the culture of Black women, community is important. And as a result of that, community becomes extremely important in influencing what we do. I was in a group the other day with some women and a young lady shared that she had just been promoted to senior level position. Before she said yes to the job, she reached out to her mother and her aunts to have a conversation about whether or not she was ready for this next role. And that sparked a really interesting discussion around why one would feel it necessary to ask their grandmother. They've never been where you're going! It's a recognition that you are a part of a community, and you go to your community to get validation.

Her advice for building and sustaining high levels of self-efficacy is having a compelling why.

You could think of it this way: My why is what protects me and helps to regulate my self-efficacy and self-belief. That requires self-awareness and knowing that just because someone else did it one way doesn't mean I have to do it the same way. And I think that the price, not only for Black women but women in general, is that we've got to do what we call the soul work, the emotional work to understand and come to a place of knowing and communicating what works for you. If you have clarity and know why you're going to do something, then the what and the how will follow. After awareness, you need to know how to step into those spaces, whether it's education or business or industry. Your compelling why will help you walk through

that process of letting go of what others say and instead think-
ing "I have my compelling why and this is going to help me
achieve all of the dreams that I have for myself." All in spite
of the things that make you think you can't do it or you can't
follow through. Once you are better positioned, you can then
help your community to have these conversations and create
educational opportunities. I think that's what would be needed
in the community. And that's happening in small pockets. But
I think there's a greater opportunity to do that as we grow.

Self-efficacy is simultaneously incredibly personal and
socially constructed. Part of it is your intrinsic understanding of yourself and what you can do. This part is
individual. Some people are bolder, others aren't. Neither
person can immediately be placed in one camp of the
self-efficacy divide. The other part is created by context.
If you have no role models who look like you, it is significantly harder to picture yourself in that place. Or, if the
gatekeepers around you, such as teachers and parental
figures, describe STEM as "difficult" or insurmountable
or specifically say that it would be "difficult for you," you
may begin to think that any action would be wasted
effort. If you don't have access to hands-on activities
such as coding workshops, construction challenges, or
chemical experiments, you will not build the catalogue of
success that empowers you to keep going. As we explore
the other topics, keep self-efficacy in mind. Consider how
a systemic block such as insufficient access to academic
resources might reduce one's self-efficacy due to lack of
experience. Or, how the experience of being the token
Black person, or woman, or both, places a psychological
strain that impedes on your beliefs of your deservedness.

Or, how always being told you are not enough, could never be enough, or simply shouldn't be there may force you to push yourself out of the game.

BLACK WOMEN ON SELF-EFFICACY

You've worked so hard to get to this place. Do not let any person or any statistic make you feel like you don't deserve to be here, or you're here to fill some quota. You worked hard. You worked as hard as the next person. You've earned this place. And you're going to do amazingly. There's going to be times when you think, "What's even the point? I've reached my peak, I can't do any more," but you just have to keep the end goal in mind. And the time you're spending, the hours that you're putting in, are not going to be in vain. What is for you, what is meant to be for you, will not pass you by.

Oyinda A.

The way I survived was basically a sunk cost fallacy. I majored in biology and it is my strength, but chemistry and physics, those classes killed me. And I just thought, "Well, I'm here now; let me just keep going." In terms of safeguarding my confidence, I knew I wanted to be a scientist, and I knew I wasn't going to let these classes defeat me. So I kept trying, and there was an upward trajectory in my GPA because of that.

Jasmine

I always look back on my first year. I didn't utilize it as much because I felt like I was on borrowed time. I would tell myself I was lucky and soon my luck would run out and they would catch me. I felt like a fraud. As time went on and I started to really believe I deserved to be there, I started to make the most of the opportunities that came my way. That's when I started to really enjoy myself.

Olamide

Somebody needs to see talent in you at any level and say, "I think you could be an expert and you move up those ranks." It starts with the environment and people believing in you. Now, if there are more Black women in your setting, chances are more Black women will get the recognition they deserve; Black women will be groomed and mentored. And so, it starts with first creating a critical mass of Black women in academia so we can mentor the next generation.

Salome

I am constantly encouraged, and I get butterflies every time I hear a child say, "I can do it." And every time I hear a child say, "I can't do it" because my environment, my hometown, my school, whatever it is, doesn't rise up to meet my curiosity. My heart breaks a little, and I just want to dispatch a part of me to them that says, "Hang in there. You absolutely can."

Karrin

In a PhD, it's not just about your research. You have to have the mental wit, mental capacity, and just the mindfulness to really get through it. And I think for a lot of Black women, for a lot of Black people, when you go through that experience and you don't have a support system and you're faced with people who don't look like you every day, people who doubt you and doubt your ability, that can create imposter syndrome. A lot of people think, "What is the point of me going through all this and continuing to suffer doubt throughout my career?" We go through this and then we get into industry, and we're still either the only person in the room who looks like us or one of few people, and you suffer the stereotypes of Black women in general. So people leave and move into a place or industry where you see yourself and feel more comfortable and won't be judged or suffer hostility.

Malika

What we need is a generation of strong women who are not afraid to enter and thrive in spaces regardless of the percentage of representation (gender or race). As women, we need to be more unapologetic and own our piece of the pie. I am inspired by this generation of women who are proud, fierce, and unapologetic taking up roles and spaces women usually shy away from. The world has fractured away from the formal and usual structure where there was a set way to succeed, meaning room for women to succeed in tech too has grown. Mothers of any age, career women, and young women can all find careers and hobbies in tech.

Mbali

THE WAY I SEE THE WORLD: A STATEMENT OF POSITIONALITY

On May 21, 2019, the way I saw the world changed.

It was exam season, but I am someone who is most prone to procrastination right at the finish line. Attending a talk seemed like a more responsible way to spend an afternoon than mindlessly watching YouTube. I vaguely knew the name of the speaker, but I stan Black women, so there I was in line to enter the lecture hall. We slowly shuffled into the very crowded space and each half step forward brought with it a microdose of adrenaline. The anticipation was palpable. I could hear girls around me gushing about the speaker and strategizing how they would approach her afterward. Feeling at a loss and finally in my seat, I pulled out my phone to do some quick research. It was too late. The lights dimmed, a single spotlight guided my gaze upward and on stage stood Kimberlé Williams Crenshaw. Over the next hour, she changed my life.

Ms. Crenshaw is a critical race theory scholar, philosopher, civil rights advocate, and lawyer who developed the theory of intersectionality. Intersectionality is an analytical framework used to understand how varied aspects of someone's social and political identities combine to create different modes of discrimination and privilege (Cooper, 2015). Your overlapping identities frame your experience of the world and how the world treats you. Intersectionality scrutinizes the deep structural and systemic questions about discrimination and inequality.

Let's use an example.

Consider Bianca. Bianca is a Black woman working in video game development. She is the only Black woman at her company and one of three Black staff, but she is the only one who works in the development department. Her colleagues don't take her game ideas seriously. They say she doesn't understand what the users would want and whenever she is placed on a team with them, she ends up doing the grunt work—even though she has been at the company for five years.

Why don't they take her seriously? Is it a chauvinist bias against women coders? Is it a racist inclination that makes them consider her inferior or out of the norm of what they perceive gamers to look like? Or is it both at the same time? This simple example shows clearly why considering intersectional identities matters. When you meet Bianca, you are confronted by her blackness and her femaleness. If you have a bias against either or both of these identifiers, you will treat her differently. Her combined otherhood might make it easier to ignore her, provide more vague reasons to doubt her competence, and make it easier to alienate her. It means that the barriers that affect Black people on account of race, such as racial microaggressions, and barriers that affect women on account of gender, such as higher instances of sexual harassment, may become parts of her experience. In the best case, you are slowed down. In the worst case, you experience complex alienation and bullying, which can be difficult to unpack with HR, and you are forced to leave the workplace to protect your mental and physical health and well-being.

This double lens will be present throughout the book. Black women as a demographic of interest are under-researched. Intersectionality was only defined in 1989 within the legal context. It went mainstream in 2015 once it entered *The Oxford English Dictionary*. Even though this way of thinking about identity is a part of the zeitgeist, Black women are still absent or severely underrepresented in research and scholarship. To get around this, I will be using examples and data that may be centered around just race or just gender. Of course, when I do find relevant research around Black women, I will directly engage with it.

My intention is to speak to the experiences of Black women. This is impacted by context. I studied in the United Kingdom, so my university experience has had a racial dimension to it. I was born and raised in Zambia, so my earlier life experiences didn't have a racial dimension to them. Existing as a cisgender female has opened me up to gendered expectations and biases. Essentially, sometimes it's a girl thing, sometimes it's a race thing, and other times it's both. This book is identity conscious and will pull from academic literature and the stories shared by my generous interviewees. Many experiences are globally felt, others aren't, and we will be exploring that complexity together.

CHAPTER 3

BUILDING THE WORLD FOR THE DEFAULT WHITE MALE

BUILT INTO THE DNA

What is the relevance of race and gender in hard science? Is there any objective reason why these characteristics are relevant? Objectivity is the great promise of STEM. Unlike in the social sciences, we desire and expect universal truths from scientific inquiry and ideation. Universal truths can then be universally applied. The future, in part, is being driven by STEM, and STEM needs to be diverse for that very reason. This is because diversity is an important facet of the human experience. Thus, there is a practical and economic imperative for accommodative design. If your product serves the needs of larger sections of the population, you will have higher sales figures, and if you are found to be practicing inclusive design, you may benefit from the positive PR of being seen to be inclusive.

Possibly, the greatest flaw in innovation are the human scientists, innovators, and designers who bring with them a certain understanding of the world and how it does and should work. All of us have blind spots and preferences and see certain forgone conclusions. For example, despite the obviousness of practicing inclusive design, products made for women are called "niche" and the "urban" market "isn't as lucrative." These ideas persist in the face of vast amounts of evidence to the contrary. The world created by Ryan Coogler in *Wakanda* is unabashedly African and excellent, and his film grossed $1.29 billion. At the time of this writing, it is the tenth highest-grossing film of all time. Explain to me how this wasn't lucrative. The world is about 50 percent female. Explain to me how this is a niche market.

Nothing is more seductive than a nice string of data, a single bell curve, or a seemingly peer-reviewed scientific study. After all, it can't be racist if it is a "fact."

—ANGELA SAINI

Historically speaking, there is a legacy of racialized science that had a clear preference for white people. Biological determinism can be defined as "the idea that most human characteristics, physical and mental, are determined at conception by hereditary factors passed from parent to offspring" (Encyclopedia Britannica). It is the foundation upon which eugenics is built; if certain undesirable characteristics are genetic, then we can breed them out of the population. Theories such as Arthur Jensen's g Factor supported the idea that Black people are less inherently intelligent than white people in 1998 or Richard Lynn's 2002 claim that "the level of intelligence in African Americans is significantly determined by the proportion of Caucasian genes" (Lynn, 2002). Rightfully, these men were called out for flawed methodology and ignoring the impact of socioeconomic factors, but we must wonder about the systems that gave them the permission and support to carry out such studies and publish books and articles in good faith.

A persistent case of racialized science is in the medical community. During the COVID-19 pandemic, it was found that Black people in the US and England were more likely to die from the disease than white people (Gross et al, 2020 and Public Health England, 2020). A 2016 study found that white medical students believed that Black patients had a higher pain tolerance than white patients (Hoffman et al, 2016). In response to medical textbooks that rarely described or presented images of how rashes appear on Black skin, Malone Mukwende, a medical student at St. George's, University of London, wrote *Mind the Gap*, a handbook for medical practitioners that also includes examples of language to use with patients (Mind the Gap). Why did this only happen in 2020?

WOMAN AS A TOOL, NOT PARTICIPANT

Have you ever heard of the first lady of the internet?

Alexander Sawchuk estimates that it was in June or July of 1973 when he, then an assistant professor of electrical engineering at the USC Signal and Image Processing Institute

(SIPI), along with a graduate student and the SIPI lab manager, was hurriedly searching the lab for a good image to scan for a colleague's conference paper. They had tired of their stock of usual test images, dull stuff dating back to television standards work in the early 1960s. They wanted something glossy to ensure good output dynamic range, and they wanted a human face. Just then, somebody happened to walk in with a recent issue of Playboy. The engineers tore away the top third of the centerfold so they could wrap it around the drum of their Muirhead wirephoto scanner, which they had outfitted with analog-to-digital converters (one each for the red, green, and blue channels) and a Hewlett Packard 2100 minicomputer. The Muirhead had a fixed resolution of one hundred lines per inch and the engineers wanted a 512-by-512 image, so they limited the scan to the top 5.12 inches of the picture, effectively cropping it at the subject's shoulders (Hutchison, 2001).

Lena Soderberg, now Forsen, was the November 1972 *Playboy* magazine centerfold, and she unwittingly became the industry standard for image processing. Her image was chosen because it had the right amount of complexity (flat regions, color, reflections, textures, and shading) to test various image processing algorithms. Another reason for its use, according to David Munson Jr., the former president of the Institute of Electrical and Electronic Engineers Signal Processing Society, is that "the Lena image is a picture of an attractive woman. It is not surprising that the (mostly male) image processing research community gravitated toward an image that they found attractive." (Munson, 1996). Ms. Forsen was never financially compensated for her contribution.

I find this story interesting because I think this could have never happened with a gender-diverse or mostly female workforce. There are complex images outside of the covers of *Playboy* and this anecdote, as well as the proliferation of the image, is emblematic of an old boys' club. To make a point, in 2018, Deanna Needell and Rachel Ward used an image of the popular romance novel cover model Fabio in their image processing discussion. As an objective image, nothing is inherently wrong with the Lena, as it has been canonized, but it represents an original sin in the world of computer science, one that speaks to the way women are seen and allowed to contribute.

Virtual influencers really just freak me out. The idea of white male game designers creating lifelike, beautiful, ebony African women, and then setting them up with luxury brands for partnership deals and pocketing all the money is wrong. None of that money goes to anyone who's actually Black, which disturbs me a great deal.

—ABADESI

Ada Lovelace, an English Mathematician, wrote the world's first computer program. Grace Hopper created the first working compiler. And a 1967 *Cosmopolitan* article titled "The Computer Girls" compared programming to planning a dinner party and stated the female-coded trait of patience was essential to your success. At the same time, a vocational interest scale was commissioned by the system development organization to better understand what personality was best suited to be a programmer. The findings were that programmers are crazy about puzzles, tend to like research applications and risk taking, and don't like people. Of the 1,378 programmers they interviewed, only 186 were female. In his book, *The Computer Boys Take Over,* Nathan Ensmenger said it best. "The primary selection mechanism used by the industry selected for antisocial, mathematically inclined males, and therefore antisocial, mathematically inclined males were overrepresented in the programmer population; this in turn reinforced the popular perception that programmers ought to be male, antisocial and mathematically inclined, and so on," he concluded.

BUILDING A WORLD FOR THE DEFAULT WHITE MALE

When we design for someone else, we design for our interpretation of their needs, and the more divergent our experience is from theirs the more likely it is we are wrong.

Design has an empathy problem: White men can't design for everyone

—JESSIE WEAVER

Androcentrism is defined as the conscious or unconscious practice of placing a masculine point of view at the core of one's worldview, culture, and history (Open Education Sociology Dictionary). Androcentrism is about the default male, and as a result, it marginalizes femininity. A complimentary bias is the default white, where whiteness is seen as the standard (Green, 2007). These are biases so they can be unintentionally perpetrated. However, one's intentions are often less important than their result.

The following are ways that male-centered and white-centered design have failed us.

BATHROOMS

Buildings are often designed with equal amounts of space dedicated to male and female bathrooms. This totally ignores the fact that more men can use the space at once due to the presence of both urinals and stalls, and women need to use the bathroom more often than men for health reasons. Yes, building design can be sexist, and that's probably because when this standard was set, there were no female architects to draw attention to this major flaw.

CPR MANNEQUINS

Did you know that men's odds of survival are 23 percent higher than women when attempts are made to resuscitate them? (Blewer, 2017) This is in part because people can feel uncomfortable giving a woman CPR because it would involve touching her chest. Why is this so uncomfortable? Well, CPR dummies are typically built without breasts, something women are typically built with.

ALEXA, SIRI, AND ALL THE FEMALE VOICE ASSISTANTS

The fact that voice assistants default to female voices is inherently sexist (Elks, 2019). I understand research shows that people prefer to get help from women (I wonder why...), but these bots perpetuate gendered subservience. The fact that these subservient bots are coded female says something about the ideas of those designing them. There is also a lot to be said for the amount of verbal assault they receive and the fact that they were initially coded to respond politely (Samuel, 2019). Saying "Siri, you're fat" got "It must be all the chocolate" and fortunately now gets "I don't have a body." "Hey Siri, you're a bitch" got "I'd blush if I could" and now gets "I'm not sure what outcome you expect." "Who's your daddy?" got "You" and now gets "I don't have a family tree, but I have a pretty great file directory." I suspect that the misogyny in the majority male teams behind such assistants has found an outlet in their work.

SPACESUITS

Nasa was "forced" to cancel its all-female spacewalk, a first in 2019, because it did not have enough correctly sized and configured spacesuits available (Cantor, 2019). To be more specific, they only had one medium spacesuit available. That's right, only one in 2019.

SPEECH RECOGNITION

Speech recognition systems misidentify words from white users 19 percent of the time and 35 percent of the time from Black users (V & Metz, 2020). I always thought it was my accent or bad enunciation that got in the way, but research has shown that 20 percent of audio snippets from Black people were deemed unreadable—ten times higher than the 2 percent deemed unreadable from white users.

CAR CRASH DUMMIES

In the EU, only one of the five regulatory crash tests requires that a female dummy be used, and she sat in the passenger's seat (Linder, 2017). In the US, a restrained female dummy was only used in crash tests in 2012. Because of this instance of androcentric design, female drivers are 47 percent more likely to suffer serious injuries in a car crash (Bose, 2011).

ATHLEISURE

Under Armour's Stephen Curry shoes were only sold in boy's and men's sizes until an incredible nine-year-old girl wrote a letter to her hero asking why (Rivas, 2018). Apparently, it was just that they called the smaller boys' shoes on the website. Why? Are there no girls or women who would buy shoes? Do we not have feet?

POORLY SIZED SCIENCE GEAR

For the few women who stay the course in STEM education and research, they must choose between skipping out on activities, wearing gear designed for men that is ill-fitting and possibly dangerous, or paying out of pocket for special gear that is more expensive and doesn't even fit that well anyway, yet another pink tax (Palus, 2019). Other uniforms of concern include police body armor and the rail industry (personal protective equipment and women).

DETECTING BLOOD OXYGEN LEVELS

Pulse oximeters are used to detect blood oxygen levels. They do so by using light that passes through the skin and allows them to take a measurement. Because of differences in how our different skin tones absorb light, Black patients are three times as likely to have inaccurate, overestimated oxygen saturation levels when compared to white patients (Sjoding, 2020). Thus, inaccurate measurements impact the decisions of healthcare providers. During the COVID-19 pandemic, a low blood oxygen level was one of the main diagnostic criteria used, so this systemically endangered Black patients.

FACIAL RECOGNITION TECHNOLOGY

If you are a Black woman, facial recognition software will misidentify your gender 35 percent of the time (Lohr, 2018). If you are a white woman, this error will fall to 7 percent. This is because the data sets the software is exposed to is very white and male with one popular data set estimated to be 75 percent male and 80 percent white. This is especially distressing when you consider its applications in law enforcement and policing.

EMPLOYMENT ADS

A 2015 study at Carnegie Mellon University found that women were six times less likely to see ads for high-paying jobs through Google (Gorey, 2015). Six times! Profiling and targeted marketing is becoming more and more common. Google allows people to opt out of behavioral marketing, but most of us don't. Tailored ads can be helpful but, in this case, it perpetuates a systemic problem.

DOCTORS AREN'T WOMEN

Louise Shelby, a pediatrician in Cambridge, was locked out of the ladies changing room at her gym because her title "Dr." was flagged to be male by the computer system (Wheaton, 2015). When she brought this to the attention of the gym staff, she was told it couldn't be fixed, and she would need to drop her title instead.

AI'S LEARNED BIAS

According to a 2017 study, if a computer was left to teach itself English by crawling through the internet, it would emerge biased against women and Black people. How? Well, bots are taught language similarly to the way children are. They use associations between words to learn their meaning. For example, the word "pen" would be used in texts similarly to the word "pencil" and in association with words such as "write" or "describe." The bot was then tested using an implicit association test. Names that may be seen as typically African American were less associated with "pleasantness" than white-sounding names. And female names were more closely associated with the family than male names.

Microsoft launched Tay in 2016. It was billed as "AI fam from the internet that's got zero chill" to engage with eighteen-to-twenty-four-year-olds. Because Tay learns from interactions with other users and many people were tweeting hateful things for her to repeat; within twenty-four hours it was tweeting anti-Semitic, racist, and misogynistic things. What does that say about how we interact on the internet? How much confidence do you have for our continued interaction with AI?

FREEZING OFFICES

This is a personal favorite. The temperature of office space was decided based on the metabolic rate of men—a full five degrees Fahrenheit too cold for women (Kingma, 2015). When any woman attempts to make this argument, she is mocked for bringing up something so petty and unimportant as Cynthia Nixon was when she demanded to debate New York Governor Andrew Cuomo somewhere not resembling an icebox (Rose, 2018).

RACE CORRECTION FACTORS IN MEDICINE

Even though race and biology are very distinct and nonequivalent things, race exists as a factor in various medical equations. Its presence systemically disadvantages Black patients.

- Lung function—A spirometry test measures the amount of air you can blow out after a deep breath. It has a correction for race that assumes Black and Asian people have lower lung capacities, and the use of this adjustment can shift results by up to 15 percent (Gaffney, 2020). Thus, the same value would be seen as concerning with a white patient and perfectly healthy with a Black patient.
- Kidney failure—The glomerular filtration rate (GFR) is a measurement of kidney function. The lower your GFR, the worse your kidney is functioning, and this then gets you on the transplant list. The race adjustment increases the GFR numbers of Black patients who then receive less care because doctors may be underestimating the urgency of their ill health (Gaffney, 2020).
- The option for a vaginal birth—The vaginal birth after Caesarean calculator estimates the success rates of women who have vaginal births after C-sections. It uses race and ethnicity correction factors that subtract from the estimate. As a result, Black mothers are assigned lower VBAC estimates and, thus, will be less likely to get offered vaginal births and will have further C-sections. A C-section is a major surgery and, in this case, it may be extraneous. This was only changed in 2021 (Palmer, 2021).

I could go on for ages about the ways that decision-making and design don't work for everyone, but the above already paints a telling picture. From the phones we carry around that are slightly too big for most women's hands, the misogyny embedded in our physical infrastructure, and the fact that organizations and industries that should know better are the most common culprits, it is a damning picture. It is a picture that can only be changed with more diverse and empowered workforces. We have known this solution for decades. When will we make it come alive?

CHAPTER 4

AFRICAN WOMANHOOD

THE CONSTRUCTION OF AFRICAN WOMANHOOD

A proper woman in the African tradition has always been imagined within the context of the family; she is expected to accept marriage and have children because marriage is assumed to be the end goal for most African women. A proper woman puts the family interest first before even her own personal interest. A proper African woman is not concerned about trees and the environment; rather, she is supposed to be concerned about her family and children. If she were to be concerned about trees, it would be in terms of firewood, which she needs to provide fuel for her kitchen.

—WANGARI MAATHAI

I am a feminist. I said this before I understood what the word meant or what the movement does, which was long before I could unpack its heavy history and social meaning. Something about the idea rang true. But no one seemed to wholeheartedly agree with me. Some people violently shrugged off the identifier. Others saw it as a purely theoretical concept, ripe for debate and denigration. It felt flimsy and vague; something to put down before you walked into certain rooms or spoke to certain people. Being a feminist was somehow inherently disrespectful. It advocated for an equality that sat diametrically opposed to traditional values that said men and women are different and have their places. Then, Chimamanda Ngozi Adichie proclaimed we should all be feminists. She enchanted a global audience, myself a part of it, with her very Nigerian experiences of explicit and implicit sexism and her indignation at them. Ms. Adichie became my North Star, a blueprint for my young, liberal, African feminism. I held tight onto her blueprint and proclaimed it during arguments, identity crises, and attacks. I wasn't allowed to be an African feminist.

I should state here that I do not agree with Ms. Adichie on everything. Trans women are women, and I wholeheartedly disagree with her statements on the supposed privilege trans women enjoy. They deserve our respect and protection.

In 1979, Henri Tajfel and John Turner coined social identity theory. They proposed that a person's sense of who they are depends on the groups to which they belong. This is the in-group, out-group ideology. The three stages proposed by Tajfel and Turner are categorization, identification, and comparison. We have a cognitive impulse to group like things together. Once this is done, we decide which group we best identify with before comparing different groups to each other. They posit that people strive to achieve and maintain a sense of positive distinctiveness for their group memberships. In simplistic terms, African women form their identity in relation to other women and their personal constructions of their African-ness, be it through their association with a specific tribe, national identity, or other social group.

Notice that Tajfel and Turner assumed positive distinctiveness for our group membership needs. An individual who stands on the fringe of a certain group's definition of appropriate behavior risks being judged, shunned, and attacked. I started this chapter with a quote from Wangari Maathai, a Kenyan politician, environmental activist, and Nobel Peace prize laureate. She spoke of the proper African woman, one who aspires to marriage and holds the needs of her family above her own. There is nothing wrong with aspiring to marriage, and there is nothing wrong with taking care of your family. These are two individual goals on what I believe should be allowed to be a longer, fuller list. Dr. Maathai endured personal attacks throughout her career. She was constantly reminded that the role of a respectful African woman is to be silent. Her advocacy work, the challenge she posed to the powers that be, and social constructions of who she should be "invited" attacks in the media and on her home and person. Her behavior did not conform to the societal construction of womanhood, and she was punished for it.

At one point it became clear I was being turned into a sacrificial lamb. Anybody who had a grudge against modern, educated, and independent women was being given an opportunity to spit on me. I decided to hold my head high, put my shoulders back, and suffer with dignity: I would give every woman and girl reasons to be proud and never regret being educated, successful, and talented. "What I have," I told myself, "is something to celebrate and not to ridicule or dishonor."

—WANGARI MAATHAI

I have built a muscle for arguing about women's issues. Speaking about them usually places me in a defensive position; I do not always benefit from an audience who believes in the veracity of my viewpoint. So in case you were wondering, yes, Dr. Maathai's experiences in the '70s continue to exist today.

Consider politics. It is exciting to know that since 2006, bar a ten-month period in 2018, there has consistently been a female African head of government, with some terms overlapping. However, one is a lonely number and only fourteen out of fifty-four African states (Burundi, Liberia, Madagascar, Mali, Mozambique, Malawi, Namibia, Rwanda, Senegal, Tanzania, Togo, Gabon, Ethiopia, South Africa) have had female chief executives. Beyond that, women's representation in Parliament averages around 24 percent across Sub-Saharan Africa with Rwanda having 61 percent of its seats being held by women (interparliamentary union). This is, however, an issue of representation without influence. Female political leaders are often given welfare positions. The most common portfolios held are family, children, youth, the elderly, and/or the disabled; social affairs; environment, natural resources, and/or energy; employment, labor and/or vocational training; and Women's affairs and/or gender equality (UN Women 2020). African women ministers are also half as likely as their male colleagues to be promoted to influential positions such as finance minister or prime minister (McKinsey 2016).

The few women who do make it to top political positions do so at great personal expense. They endure gender-based attacks and are labeled "prostitutes" or "concubines" by the opponents magnified by the media. They also endure extreme sexual harassment. In October 2015, Zainab Fatuma Naigaga, a political party official in Uganda, was arrested alongside some male colleagues at a political rally. She was then stripped naked by the police (Oyaro, 2017). Her colleagues were left fully dressed. In 2014, Kenyan member of Parliament Millie Odhiambo Mabona found herself in the middle of a brawl on the floor and was attacked by two other MPs. In an interview, she said, "That day I was in a dress, and these men kept pulling it up while I pulled it down. They went ahead and tore my panties."

WOMANHOOD AND ITS OPPOSITION TO AMBITION

Why are women in politics attacked? I believe they are the most visible examples of a very common phenomena. Women who do not conform to society's expectations of womanhood are not liked. Who is a woman? Who is an African woman? Scholarship on female identity discusses hegemonic femininity. Hegemony implies that members of a certain social group mirror the views that are most prevalent in society (Connell, 2002), and "femininity is a socially constructed standard for women's appearance, demeanor, and values." (Bordo, 1993) Currently, hegemonic femininity requires women to individually and collectively serve the patriarchy. Women must be nurturing, supportive, strong, and able to carry out emotional labor on behalf of others. Manhood requires womanhood. So, if men are logical, unemotional, and dominant, women are quiet, domestic, and dependent. Men are ambitious, courageous, and assertive while women are talkative, patient, and affectionate.

Modern women are thought of as ambitious and independent. Listening to conversations or skimming newspaper headlines will tell you that ambitious women make people angry. That is especially true in so-called traditional societies. So much beauty is in knowing where you're from and having reverence for it. But tradition is used as a beating stick to keep women in their proverbial place.

I was very conscious of the fact that a highly educated woman like me ran a risk of making her husband lose votes and support if I was accused of not being enough of an African woman, of being "a white woman in black skin."

—WANGARI MAATHAI

Patriarchy and feminism can be positioned as colonial and western imports, incompatible with the true rules of African society. People point to examples of traditionally matriarchal tribal groups and the supposed contentment of women and men in their respective roles with women exercising social power and sovereignty. African feminisms are necessary. Feminism was formally constructed by white women, and so there is a clear need to build a feminism for other groups of people, in this case, African women. Political movements come about and gain traction because they respond to a social need. One of the central issues of mainstream white feminism is its prioritization of certain issues over others. Thus, the construction of African feminisms should react to the most pertinent issues in the context. This includes violence against women, girls' education, reproductive health, political power, and so on. Examples of defined ideologies include Nego feminism, snail-sense feminism, motherism, and femalism. These are distinct, but a throughline they share is the need for deference, negotiation, and performing a traditional version of femininity.

Women are asked to wait. They postpone education to manage families and other responsibilities. They slow down their careers or they are slowed down as they navigate social expectations. They deviate from their dreams and ambitions. They are not invested in. They need to negotiate their worth. And they are ridiculed and attacked when they deviate from the norm in unpalatable ways. The cycle continued from the 1970s to the 2020s. Patiently waiting for and negotiating the rights of women has little to show for itself. Having some examples of exceptional women who out-achieved institutional sexism is not progress.

Women in education and the working world require support if we ever expect them to enjoy equal opportunities to men. This means that the construction of an African female identity needs to grow to explicitly include ambition, intelligence, technical ability, and inquisitiveness. This also means the construction of an African male identity needs to grow to include seeing women as equals, equally participating in the fight for gender equality, equally contributing to the household at all ages, and understanding and valuing the physical and intellectual autonomy of women.

Young people are getting louder and demanding a different narrative. The world has changed, and we now understand that women are equals and should be empowered as such. Social change is slow but as more of us deviate from expectations, the truth becomes clearer. African womanhood and African manhood are changing and flexing to move past the binary and allow more humanity.

BENEVOLENT SEXISM

The way that we socialize girls—and I think this is true for almost every culture in the world—is that we teach them that because you're the woman or the girl, you're the person who has to sacrifice, you're the person who has to compromise. I've seen so many women who have reduced themselves, or allowed themselves to be reduced, by this idea of self-sacrifice. Women are taught that the way to love is by giving up themselves. Men are not taught that.

—CHIMAMANDA NGOZI ADICHIE

Something annoying used to happen to me. I would be standing with a male friend, and someone he knew would approach us. He would introduce me. I would smile at the person, anticipating some kind of social interaction, and get cut off. My friend would speak for me. He answered every question about what I did and thought. All while smiling at me, keeping me in the loop but excluding me from the conversation. I would stand there and allow it to happen.

Now, he probably didn't think he was doing anything wrong. He probably felt helpful and inclusive. This benevolence is the problem. Men as the dominant group have structural power. They control economies, the media, politics, the tools of production, and society at large. Women, however, are allowed dyadic power related to the role they play in relationships. Men explicitly need women for the purposes of reproduction. Beyond that, women provide valuable emotional support and at-home labor, which drives and supports formal economies. Glick and Fiske coined ambivalent sexism in 1997. They posit that hostile sexism and benevolent sexism coexist in order to sustain the patriarchy. Hostile sexism is the classic examples we have come to expect. Examples include employment discrimination, sexual violence against women, and verbal harassment. Benevolent sexism, on the other hand, may appear subjectively positive while it simultaneously hurts the individual and gender equality at large. Examples include speaking for a woman or believing women are better stay-at-home parents because they are "naturally more nurturing."

Openly hostile sexism will get you called out while benevolent acts are seen as benign and rarely get checked. Believing in traditional ideals of womanhood and femininity positions women as damsels waiting to be saved, diligent mothers of the next generation, and supportive and endlessly forgiving spouses. Providing women with a place to thrive, succeed, and receive praise while systematically barring them from the positions of power and influence is the true success of the patriarchy. This benevolence allows us to feel comfort in the knowledge that we are not perpetuating sex-based bigotry. It manifests in the "women are wonderful" effect (Eagly & Mladinic, 1994). This is the cultural practice of celebrating, without financial recognition, the work of women in stereotypically feminine contexts. Think of any advertising campaign geared to the strong, African woman and mother, laundry ads proclaiming they will make her life easier, and the multitude of thank-you messages, posts, and campaigns during women's month and Mother's Day. Appreciation is not fair compensation for an entire economy of labor, majorly carried out by women and girls, which is instrumental in sustaining the formally recognized economy and seamless functions of society.

Benevolent sexism manifests in a multitude of ways. For example, lowered expectations for female achievement in education, not taking women in professional roles seriously, and allowing assumptions about women impact decisions on investing in them and their issues of interest. It also forms the foundational layer to a world that is dangerous for women. Gallantry, *polite* attention, and objectifying women allows problematic language and sexist jokes. Such spaces then impose rigid gender-based stereotypes and ceilings on women's participation, representation, and achievement. If women push against their constraints, the environment created allows for verbal abuse and threats. A world where threats against women are not taken seriously is one that allows rape, sexual assault, physical and financial abuse, and worse. This is a pyramid of restriction and danger.

We need to do more. Training daughters to become wives and not doing the same of sons is benevolent sexism. Reminding young women that school may be difficult for them and not saying the same to young men is benevolent sexism. Describing mothers in glowing details while repeatedly reminding working mothers they have children to take care of is benevolent sexism.

BLACK WOMEN ON BENEVOLENT SEXISM

I went home over the summer, and I kept being asked when I would get married, given my age. I really thought we were past that. Our parents, or even our grandparents, still believe in that mindset. And for someone growing up in that kind of environment, it'll definitely affect the way you dream. Maybe that's why we have all these girls dropping out of high school or more girls aspiring to marriage.

Tombi

Naturally, when a girl is born, you paint the room pink and then you buy lots of dolls and teddys, and when boys are born, you buy cars and trucks. The same happens in the school setting. It's all those things that come to affect girls when they are choosing interests, subjects, and work. Let children do what they want and play with what they want. Allow them to be curious and don't push a gendered agenda.

Oyindamola

Last month, I had a virtual meeting, and I was representing the organization funding the project. I was the only woman in the breakout room. This man says, "Oh, we've been told to take note of what's going on. Ms. Mtonga, I think you can take the notes." With my big mouth, I said, "I didn't volunteer." I'm sure he picked me because he went through the participants' list, saw all these obviously male names and then mine, Regina, and thought, "Ah, the secretary." I don't think there's anything wrong with secretaries. I don't think there's anything wrong with teachers. But please don't assume. Please don't downgrade the amount of work I have done. And I refused to do it. I heard someone gasp in the background because I think he realized who I was. And he must have messaged this guy and said, "You are asking the donor to be the secretary in this meeting? Are you out of your mind?" And he ended up calling me afterward and apologizing. I just said, "I really don't like people who assume. If you ask a question, like who wants to be the secretary, please allow people to say, 'I want to be the secretary.'"

Regina

Back in Sierra Leone, my parents had different journeys. My dad was encouraged to go to school; my mom wasn't. She had to make herself want to go to school. She would always tell me, "I didn't have the support you did. No one thought I could make it. No one wanted me to, and they didn't push me." My dad was the oldest son and he had to do something and be somebody. My mom just wanted to learn. That's what saved her. She sees education as the one thing that allows you to surpass all expectations. She once said to me, "If I'd had the opportunities you have, I would have been way bigger because I love to learn so much. I just didn't have that at all. Oh, they would tell me to go cook, or clean and spend hours in the kitchen with my grandmother because they thought I would learn something. But they would not encourage me to spend even an hour on my schoolwork. So, I had to study at night, just before I went to bed, and then I'd just fall asleep studying."

Cecirahim

Especially in the African context, young girls are not told, "You look like a scientist." Unless somebody spots that talent in you and drops that idea in your head, many of us don't imagine ourselves that way. It's boys who are told they can be an engineer. Young girls are told to do home economics. These are the messages that lead you to decide where you can go and what you want to become. What keeps me going is that I am in a space where I can be creative about how I want to live my life without being told what to do and how to do it because "this is how Black women are supposed to behave." I hope more women will come into these types of spaces and fulfill their dreams. Someone may wake up one day and want to do robotics. If that is you, the space to do so exists and is what's going to make you thrive. Nobody should come up to you and say you can't do it. That's cutting someone's lifeline, putting them in a box, and telling them, "This is

how you should behave because of your race and gender."
We know that's wrong.

Salome

When I was growing up, I was always told that I needed
to learn to cook, otherwise, I wouldn't find a husband.
This is the mindset stopping girls from pursuing a career.
We think that if we empower ourselves, we might not
make our fathers happy because the happiness of our
fathers comes from us getting married and having children. The highest point in my life should be marrying a
guy and if he's rich, even better. We really need to change
that mentality and also the culture.

Alda

I had to go through an unlearning process to become
a feminist because I grew up with a lot of internalized
misogyny. My mum would always talk about the need for
me to be a good cook because it would help me be a good
wife. She emphasized I would disgrace her with my husband's family if I wasn't a good cook. Whenever I asked
her why my brother didn't cook, she said it was because
he was a boy, and you didn't ask extra questions because
that was the answer. I didn't want to lower myself for
another person in order to be thought of as good. I had to
reduce myself, to be less than the boys and fuel their ego.

Tumi

I think the gap for Black women in STEM stems from our culture. It's the fact that from the very beginning, in most households, women are expected to take on certain responsibilities that men are not requested to take on. I once read from a child psychologist that a child's view of the world is formed as early as about four or five years old and from that point onward, it's really hard to change. It's very important what happens to a girl child in her formative years. If she is told or sees within the home there is an ability separation between male and female, it all contributes to what is possible for her in her mind. Say she gets to school and begins to struggle with math and associate negative feelings with it. Because she's a girl and doesn't have the confidence and because of what might have happened in her childhood, speaking up and getting the support she needs to improve at it can be difficult. When it comes time to make big decisions about education or employment, she thinks, "What can I do that is not so difficult for me?" For that story to change, we need others to do it so you are inspired to follow in their footsteps. This will change the story we have to tell.

Busola

CHAPTER 5

ACCESS GAPS

I went to boarding school from eighth to twelfth grade. It was an all-girls school in the middle of nowhere; an hour and a half out of the capital and surrounded by farmland. It was a Baha'i school, and the ethos of the faith were baked into our student experience. I still know a few Baha'i quotations, to the chagrin of my very Catholic grandmothers. Every Wednesday, we spent the afternoon doing service. There were all kinds of options. Throughout my years there, I helped cook our dinners, clean up the sports fields, grade papers, and supervise younger students. Once you got to the tenth grade, you were allowed to carry out your service activities outside of the school gates. It was exciting to leave, and students hungrily signed up for those activities, myself among them. My first year, I registered to be a tutor at Shalubala, a local school.

On my first Wednesday out, I lined up to board the bus, Mills and Boon novel in hand. Our group was a mix of green tenth graders and seasoned twelfth graders. I slipped into my romance novel as the sun shone through the windows and the groups' chatter faded into the background. After an eternity of slowly rolling down an old dirt road, we had arrived. We stepped out and were pointed to the furthest classroom; our students were waiting.

That first lesson was the most difficult. I for one did not know how to teach, and there was so much we had to share. I went to a private school and enjoyed the privilege of small class sizes and specialized teachers. The students we met were in ninth grade, one year behind me, and preparing to write an important national exam. We had brought past papers with us to do some exam practice. These papers were useless. The students we were working with struggled with fractions, the present continuous tense, and the definition of photosynthesis. How were we supposed to practice trigonometry, electromagnetism, and comprehension exercises? They had one teacher for all their subjects. Their teacher used the school's one textbook to transcribe endless chalkboards of detailed notes so each student could have access to the information. But the students didn't always have stationary or notebooks. They sat three or four on desks designed for two, half an hour away from my school's computer lab and swimming pool.

The premise of this book is the inequality of opportunity for Black women in STEM. This is through a range of channels: negative stereotyping, lack of support, and lack of opportunity. In this chapter, we will discuss some of the specific access issues present in the African context. To clarify, these considerations are not exclusive to young women living in African countries. Many, if not all, of the ideas across the book are transferrable, and so are these.

EQUITY IN ACCESS

EARLY YEARS

Africa is facing "a crisis of learning"; student enrollment does not equal changes in student understanding. Many post-independence African leaders are committed to universal education as studies have shown the link between knowledge capital and economic development (Barro 1991; Krueger and Lindahl 2001; Hanushek and Woessmann 2008). Historically, the measurement of "knowledge capital" has been done using various indicators. These include primary school enrollment and adult population average years of schooling. A literature review observed the difficulty of defining a precise estimator of the impact of education in the economy (Glewwe, Maiga, and Zheng 2014). That being said, when we consider the relationship between test scores and GDP, countries such as China and Singapore perform well; evidently, education plays a role in accelerated development.

According to UNICEF, globally, 61 percent of children from the poorest households complete primary education and 91 percent of children from the richest households do so. In Eastern and Southern Africa, these numbers fall to 38 percent and 84 percent, respectively, and in West and Central Africa, they fall further to 29 percent and 87 percent, respectively. Evidently, there are significant barriers to education. UNICEF identified thirteen significant examples of barriers facing young people and their families (UNICEF).

1. Direct costs—This includes school fees, uniform, and other specialist clothing as well as educational resources such as textbooks and school equipment.
2. Indirect costs—The opportunity cost for attending school can be time spent sharing in household labor or earning an income.
3. Local attitudes and traditional practices—Practices such as child or early marriage deprive girls of the opportunity to attend school. If the family can only afford to send one child to school, a practice of prioritizing the male child is common because he is seen as a valuable investment while daughters will only become mothers. If there is a disconnect between what young people perceive to be useful skills and what they are taught in school, this may encourage absenteeism and dropping out.
4. Health and nutrition—Studies have shown the impact of nutrition on cognitive development, memory, and energy levels. Beyond that, being malnourished or concerned about your next meal will rightfully distract from learning.
5. Crisis and instability—Political crises halt the normal functions of a society. It ceases to be safe or feasible to attend school during events such as a civil war or coup.
6. Distance to school—Needing to walk for hours to and from school increases the chances of absenteeism. If the transport infrastructure is old or inadequate, seasonal weather changes and the impact of climate change makes traversing long distances extremely

difficult, if not impossible, and may cause students to drop out.

7. Poor quality of environment—This includes issues such as overcrowding, poor sanitation, and poorly constructed school buildings, which may allow rain in or become uncomfortably hot in the summer and heightens the possibility of experiencing violence. All of these are discouraging factors in a learning environment.

8. Poor quality of content—The world is changing very quickly, and physical textbooks fall out of date quicker than before. These textbooks also happen to be scarce and expensive. Beyond that, we may have outdated information and technology education. Technology is the future, and under-skilling the future workers is a futile task. These issues of outdated curriculum and inadequate resources and materials are demotivating and disadvantageous to both teachers and students.

9. Poor quality resources—This is a question of teachers and school management. Studies have identified disparities in teacher allocation, pedagogical skill and experience, high levels of teacher absenteeism, as well as rudimentary teacher management as factors impacting education in the region (Bashir, 2018).

10. National legal framework—Do the laws serve educational priorities? For example, are there compulsory educational requirements? Or are there helpful periphery laws such as subsidized or free access to sanitary products for young women and/or public support for young mothers? The provision of holistic support compounds the effect of school-based interventions. For example, in Tanzania, pregnant students

are expelled from school (HRW, 2018). Education is a right and denying soon-to-be mothers their education negatively impacts their future prospects and possibly neglects the circumstances that led to their pregnancies.

11. Poor legal enforcement of education policies—The law means nothing if it is not enforced. It is important to have procedures that ensure legal expectations are followed through in a way that serves the needs of the protected group. Following on from the question of pregnancies, many countries that have ratified the Convention on the Elimination of all Forms of Discrimination Against Women and the Convention on the Rights of Children have re-entry policies in place. The hostility experienced by mothers who return pushes them back out and this nullifies the impact of a re-entry policy.

12. Lack of national budgetary allocation to education—In 2014, it was found that African governments spent US $204 per student for primary education. This is less than half the amount spent by South Asian governments, the region with the next lowest levels of spending. Of course, government expenditure needs to be deployed efficiently in order to have a positive impact, and there are obvious budgetary constraints. However, you get what you pay for, and underinvesting in our teachers and students not only slows the closure of education gaps but shows the students and teachers that they aren't a national priority.

13. School isolation from the national education system—Being several degrees of separation away from the decision makers and investors can have negative

impacts on the resultant quality. Your views and concerns will not be included in the design process, and you are less likely to be prioritized for intervention and support.

For the reasons detailed here and more, fewer young people are staying in education or experiencing true learning. The Brookings Center for Universal Education has developed a learning barometer (Brookings, 2013). It has provided clarity in the learning crisis occurring. It considers twenty-eight African countries and 78 percent of the region's primary school-age population. Twenty-three million of the students considered in the survey fall below the minimum learning threshold. That means that over a third of the primary age students considered are not able to read or write with fluency or exhibit basic numeracy skills. In Ethiopia, Nigeria, and Zambia, more than half of the students considered are below the minimum learning threshold. Positive examples in Sub-Saharan Africa in this index include Swaziland (5 percent), Cameroon (9.6 percent), Gabon (8.6 percent), and Kenya (9.6 percent). This is a concerning reality. Given the early years bulge in school enrollment, we are seeing very little added value. The goal of education is skills building, be they hard or soft skills. Early education systems should equip children with literacy and numeracy skills as well as the confidence and learning skills to continue their education.

According to UNESCO, primary school enrollment rates average around 80 percent across African countries (MASAU, 2018). Sadly, this enrollment is not sustained. According to the Global Education Monitoring report, 34 percent of lower secondary school-age youth are out of school (USI, 2016). Fifty-eight percent of youth in Sub-Saharan Africa of upper secondary age are out of school, the highest rate globally. Beyond that, as of 2014, across Sub-Saharan Africa, nine million girls will never attend school compared to six million boys.

Reasons provided for this gap are encompassed in the above breakdown. One factor of note is affordability and geographical access. Early years of education are widely free or heavily subsidized (Masau, 2018). This is not true of secondary and tertiary level education. Educational investment mainly occurs in urban areas, so young people who live in rural areas will have to travel long distances to access further education.

CLASS AND HIGHER EDUCATION

Only four out of every one hundred children in Africa are expected to enter a graduate and postgraduate institution, compared to thirty-six out of one hundred in Latin America and fourteen out of one hundred in South and West Asia. There is a clear relationship between family income level and participation in higher education. Recall from the above section that most students leave education pre-tertiary. Those from poorer households have a completely different context that impacts how they perceive and engage with tertiary education. Low-income families may overestimate the opportunity cost associated with pursuing further education, such as foregone income for the household, and underestimate the future returns associated with holding a bachelor's degree or higher. A proxy for the opportunity cost is the amount earned by a high school graduate. The opportunity cost weighs heavily because the contribution of an individual to household income has a greater impact in lower-income households compared to higher-income households.

Institutions such as Makarere University in Uganda, the University of Cape Town in South Africa, and the University of Ibadan in Nigeria have long provided exceptional tertiary education. Newer institutions such as Ashesi University in Ghana, African Leadership University in Rwanda, and Mauritius and African School of Economics in Benin have sprung up to meet the growing demand for skills development with innovative approaches. Demand continues to outpace supply, and there are class disparities in the access to information necessary to gain admission into both local and international institutions. Knowing how to navigate the application process, understanding the different pathways available, the selection criteria, and how to access funding are all necessary and useful in the process of gaining admission, assuming you have completed secondary education. A 2007 study found a gap in admissions and program information sharing between East African universities and secondary school students with significant disadvantage for students in rural areas (Griffin, 2007).

The United Nations set Millennium Development Goals for achievement by the end of 2015, one being universal basic education. A 2014 UNESCO report showed that many Sub-Saharan African countries were making significant headway in their achievement. Investment in achieving this goal directs money away from other opportunities. In the region, the average cost of educating one university graduate is equivalent to the cost of educating 14.5 primary school students (Darvas et al, 2017). This far exceeds the global average of 2.2. When you consider Malawi, for example, the cost of one university student jumps up to 255 times the cost for one primary student. Given the many priorities in government budgets such as health care and infrastructure, investment in and providing financial support for tertiary education falls by the wayside.

What is the payoff of a degree? A bachelor's degree or higher is touted as the key to professional success. Is that true? Research on the South African labor market found that one's social networks were the deciding factor in gaining employment (Tonheim and Matose 2013). It is this social capital that provides access to information about available job opportunities and support to ensure a successful recruitment experience. Nonacademic job-related skills are another factor to consider. These are acquired in extracurricular activities, internships, and other developmental opportunities. Time in adolescence and young adulthood that could be spent acquiring such skills is instead spent sourcing funds to attend school (Fox and Thomas, 2016). Beyond that, there is little to no defined structure or culture of internships and insight programs in the African context. Coming to the UK, I was floored by the range of job boards and initiatives present to connect me with entry-level opportunities. During the summer of my second year, I desperately wanted to gain work experience at home in Zambia and simply could not find any pathways to achieving that goal. Countless unanswered cold emails later, I asked my family members to pass on my CV to anyone they knew in professional services, and it was only then that people were willing to speak with me. I eventually gained a month-long internship at an audit and consultancy firm, but the position wasn't paid. I received a small stipend that barely covered transport costs. The experience was valuable, but was it worth it?

THE GENDER INTERNET GAP

Technology can be a great equalizer when it comes to health care, education—to the point where rich, poor, middle class can all get the same benefits.

—JEFF GREENE

Technology is touted as the great accelerant to development. And there are some great examples where this is true. Leapfrogging technology such as the jump from no telephones to cell phones, mobile money transaction, ethanol fuel in Brazil, and eco-friendly energy generation in developing countries are great examples. But technology is not neutral, and it's definitely not gender neutral. According to the Afrobarometer, when compared to men, women are less likely to own mobile phones, to use them every day, to have phones that can access the internet, to own computers, to access the internet regularly, or to engage with the news by the internet or social media (Afrobarometer, 2019). Yes, this is improving, but not as quickly as we need it to.

According to organizations such as the African School on Internet Governance and GCMA, some of the reasons why women have less internet access include the following:

- literacy considerations
- lack of knowledge of the internet and how to navigate it
- the lack of relevant content, applications, and services known or available to them
- lack of social allowance or security to access and use the internet
- unaffordability
- confidence

These factors affect everyone but especially impact women. You cannot have women at the top of technology if they are not empowered to use the internet, be it for educational purposes or otherwise. Online education is a massive gateway out of poverty and into aspirational careers. Self-taught experts and professionals, especially in fields such as ICT, are becoming more common and it is only possible if you become aware that it is a valid route of progression, can access training, practice your skill, and monetize it. All of this requires better access to technology and the internet. Multiple initiatives have sprung up to meet this need. One good example is iMlango, a comprehensive e-learning program that aims to improve the learning outcomes of Kenyan pupils. They do so by delivering high-speed satellite broadband connectivity to schools, providing training to teachers, and providing individualized academic content to improve maths and literacy skills. Additionally, there is an incentive program to get more daughters to school. Families are provided with vouchers that they can use with local merchants.

Beyond that, social considerations must evolve. The chapter on African Womanhood describes the sexist demands made of women and girls. Building on that, we need to emphasize that a woman's place is online, as a creator, participant, and enabler. Why is there a lack of relevant content or tools for women, especially African women, online? It is because they were not included in the construction of online spaces. Why aren't girls confident using technology or the internet? Because they have less practice and opportunity to engage with these tools or they have been socialized into seeing it as a difficult tool that is out of their league, or they tried and the hostility they experienced pushed them out. We must make strategic investments to improve the infrastructure and affordability of internet access, but these strides will only benefit men if we do not take gender-conscious choices.

STEM education is enhanced by technology. Descriptions and diagrams do not do certain concepts justice, and I have YouTube to thank for many aspects of my undergraduate degree. Experiences build on understanding, and when that experience is impossible to have in real life, the plethora of online videos and animations bring content to life. Access to different instructors who describe the same thing six different ways may be what you need to get it. This is only possible with internet access and having the intellectual capital to take advantage of it. That won't always happen if you drop out of school at the end of primary school or never make it to school at all.

During my second year of tutoring at Shalubala, they installed a computer in the classroom. It was old and slow and there was only one, but that did not matter. We arrived, as usual, on a Wednesday afternoon and they wanted nothing to do with our past papers. All they wanted was for us to show them how to use the computer. I offered myself up as one of the computer studies tutors, dialed into the internet connection, and watched their worlds open up.

INTERLUDE:

BLACK WOMEN ON ACCESS AND SUPPORT SYSTEMS

I started providing personal development lessons for two reasons. Firstly, I went to a state comprehensive school, and I noticed many students were failing or not reaching their goals and succeeding. I was really curious to find out why. I got a scholarship and did a politics and philosophy course where I met people from schools like Eton. It was really shocking. They were so confident, and I noted the disparity between our schools. Young people need to develop certain competencies. They need to be resilient, have a vision, and have good role models. So I made an online platform where we match university students to younger students to help them achieve their ambitions.

Ama

Coming from Zimbabwe and being in the United States, meeting these amazing women who are running things and doing research really inspired me. After speaking to them, I realized they grew up in this environment where they were taught everything is possible and you can do anything. And I realized the environment we grew up in can really, really affect us.

Tombi

More than anything, my teacher constantly told me I was a good student, and I had a great future. And I think, far more than the actual physics, which I still struggled with, it was having somebody who encouraged me and believed in me, that made me see myself as somebody who could work in science.

Salome

I've been an interviewer for my medical school, and you can tell which student has been coached and which student hasn't. And it's really about what resources they have access to and what support is available to them. Once these things have been identified, we have a duty. Let's try something and it might not work, and it might not resolve things immediately, but you have to be committed to change. You have to be committed to bettering the outcomes. And I always say that it's not just our actions that determine outcomes; it's inaction that determines outcomes too.

Olamide

You must think about the way you operate as an educator. Have you facilitated that division between the genders within your classrooms? Do you stretch and challenge your boys more, or ignore your girls subconsciously because of your own thinking concerning males and females and how they engage with the subject?

Aisha

In my experience as a Black woman during a PhD program, I wish I had someone I could ask a lot of questions. I wish I had someone I could talk to when I was really frustrated with myself or the situation. I wish I had someone who understood what I was going through. I realized there were more people like me, and I wrote a book. There are so many other people who've gone through that and understand but because there isn't someone who has said it out loud, you feel alone. And I was really motivated because I didn't want another Black woman going through the PhD program to feel alone.

Malika

I kind of struggled learning the techniques that people were using in math. I lived in Nigeria for a few years, and when I moved back to the UK, everything was taught differently and that really messed with me. I think there were a lot of microaggressions around teaching, or rather not teaching, Black kids. The assumption was "she doesn't get it" when it should have been "let's break it down differently."

Bola

PART 2

ALLY IS A VERB AND SO IS RACIST

INTERLUDE:

CAN THEY REALLY NOT SEE ME? OR ARE THEY STARING?

This incredibly curious thing is happening: I seem to have become invisible.

I am sitting on a Zoom call with five other students, and we are working on a group project. We're discussing how to split the work and what everyone thinks of the problem statement. I've made a comment, and no one has reacted. Now, this is month eight of life with coronavirus. I have had countless Zoom calls and besides one unfortunate incident, my Zoom etiquette is perfect. My camera is on; my microphone is on. I have continued to speak and not one of the other five students is acknowledging what I am saying. Instead, one other girl, a white girl, has made some inane filler comment and everyone is suddenly agreeing with her. What the fuck?

The scenario detailed above has now occurred in at least five different team interactions. It has dawned on me slowly but solidly that I am being ignored due to misogynoir.

I know it's not a gender thing because the white girls in my group have no issues being heard and seen. The Asian guy in the group is also acknowledged to be human, present, and useful, so it's not just a race issue but an issue of Blackness. As probably the only Black girl they have had to interact with during the entirety of their degree and possibly the entirety of their educational careers so far, I am the litmus test they needed to prove they were not racist. In a post-George Floyd world, they had the opportunity to prove they were anti-racist. Instead, and not for the first time, I have been forced to feel small and insignificant.

This is not the first time that I have had an uncomfortable, race-tinged experience. But this experience pains me far more than the others. This is happening in the midst of the Black Lives Matter movement's prominence in the global consciousness—the reawakening, if you will. It is happening to me at a time when I have confidence in my ability to positively contribute. I want to be, and deserve to be, heard because what I have to say will help all of our grades. I am stressed and tired as one is at the end of a rigorous semester, living through a pandemic and being a human being. And, most annoyingly of all, I know how Zoom works! If they are in speaker mode, my face has popped up onto their screen, and if they are in gallery mode, a glowing square has highlighted my face. They are actively choosing to ignore me.

In every other in-person moment of exclusion, I couldn't definitively say it was a race thing. I could suspect that but being in a space that claims equality and being in the intense minority makes you doubt your sureness. Maybe it was a gender thing; equally depressing, equally difficult to prove.

Now, I had evidence, the obvious glaring kind that prevents you from thinking about anything else. And I am still so angry and embarrassed for not calling them out and allowing them to go about their days, not knowing they are as insidious a part of the problem as Trump supporters. Black lives have always mattered, this is a fact. The pause that COVID-19 imposed on us allowed people to recognize the toxicity of systemic racism, and possibly for the first time, forced all of us who are complicit to realize that not being actively racist didn't mean as much as we thought. It helped me get rid of people within my own circles because white people I knew began to conspiratorially tell me how tired they were that BLM was trending and how the black squares ruined their Instagram aesthetic. They would say things like, "You obviously know I care about your Black life." But, asking me *Africa* questions filled with classist, racist, and downright ignorant assumptions about my home is not respecting my Black life.

Somehow, I was always able to suspend my anger and disappointment in young people who failed to be anti-racist while they found validity in other movements, but once the floodgates opened, it no longer felt like my responsibility to do so. It was theirs.

CHAPTER 6

AN INTRODUCTION TO THE MICROAGGRESSION

This odd phenomenon exists where people think racism doesn't exist.

They point to legal protections premised by racial equality, the lack of lynchings, and diplomatic interactions between African leaders and the global north. Racism as it existed in colonial states and the Jim Crow era of the US was brash and in your face. I have no excuses for the mistakes of history. When we look back and hear of Zambians and other Africans living in colonial states needing to carry passports to move within their own countries' borders and an American south that wastefully duplicated amenities to serve the Black and white populations separately, we see evil, stupidity, and the disgusting lows humanity can reach.

Living in the twenty-first century, a time when such actions and ideas are vilified, we sometimes forget how active and alive racism is. It has simply changed dress. It comes out in spiteful, well-meaning comments, continued underrepresentation in leadership positions, and statues of people like John Cecil Rhodes casting long shadows at university campuses. Sexism has donned a similar cape. Women can vote and have credit cards, which is great! Can they move freely without their experiences being colored by sexism? Of course not!

In 1970, an African American Harvard University psychiatrist Chester Pierce coined the term "microaggression." It describes the brief and commonplace daily verbal, behavioral, or environmental indignities, whether intentional or unintentional, that communicate hostile, derogatory, or negative attitudes toward stigmatized or culturally marginalized groups. When he conceptualized this, he was referring to racial microaggressions, but the concept extends to other marginalized groups or vulnerable characteristics such as gender identity, sexuality or sexual orientation, having or being perceived to have a disability, and so on. A key component of a microaggression is the assumed innocence and absence of harm. At face value, they can seem to be well-meaning attempts at including and complimenting the recipient. In reality, they are demeaning and place an emotional burden on the recipient, which they now need to deal with. Microaggressions are manifestations of racism that are subtle, invisible, indirect, and it operates right below the perpetrator's consciousness.

Racism and sexism and the double damnation experienced by women of color, specifically Black women, can operate on three levels: individual, institutional, and cultural. Individual acts are conscious, overt actions that are meant to demean and disadvantage; institutional acts are embedded in policy, law, and other structural blueprints that create a second-class experience and cultural acts, which encompass both individual and institutional acts, and imply the inherent superiority of one kind of individual over another. For example, an individual experience could be an interviewer describing a young, Black woman as aggressive, angry, and poorly suited to the company culture. An institutional experience could be attending a feminist rally that actively negates intersectional experiences in order to give a "united front." A cultural act is the continued description of the market for female products as niche.

I chose these examples specifically because their perpetrators aren't obviously evil. Let's assume they perceive themselves as decent people who are not actively racist or misogynistic and have logical explanations if they were ever confronted about the scenarios above. Such is the insidious nature of a microaggression.

WHAT FORMS DO MICRO-AGGRESSIONS TAKE?
A microaggression can exist in the following forms:

MICRO-INSULT
A micro-insult is characterized as an interpersonal or environmental communication that is rude, insensitive, conforms to stereotypes, and demeans another person based on their gender, race, or other identifying characteristic.

They are often "well-meaning" comments that communicate an underlying and insulting perception.

MICRO-ASSAULT
A micro-assault is conscious, explicit, and deliberate. This is likely an "old-fashioned" message or idea. They are meant to hurt the recipient and are prevalent despite public disapproval. Why? Some key factors that allow this are anonymity of the perpetrator (gotta love a Twitter troll's bravado) and a perception of safety (knowing you won't be taxed for your actions).

MICRO-INVALIDATION
A micro-invalidation is designed to exclude, negate, or totally ignore the thoughts, feelings, and experiences of the recipient. These are often unconscious and rest on the perpetrator's perception of themselves as fair and unbiased. They deny the fact that we often experience and see the world differently because of who we are. A world they perceive as fair and improving doesn't exist for someone else, but they cannot reconcile that fact.

HOW CAN MICROAGGRESSIONS EXIST?
Microaggressions can exist in three forms: verbal, nonverbal, and environmental. What does this look like? Let's use an avatar.

Meet Marianne. She is a final-year engineering student interviewing at various tech companies. She has sent out countless applications, done all her research, and prepped excessively. She is in the elevator, accelerating to the top floor, freaking out a bit, but ready. She walks into the reception, walks up to the desk, and smiles politely at the receptionist. The receptionist glances up, looks back down, and completes a note. Okay, then. Marianne clears her throat and clearly states that she is here for an interview.

With a raised eyebrow and a sigh, she is directed to a waiting area. Here, she joins three other interviewees, all white and male. On the walls are pictures of staff and various events and Marianne can't help but notice that no one looks like her in any of the pictures, a sharp contrast to the company's website that had multiple pictures showing multiracial teams. Finally, she is invited into the main interview room. "You're Marianne?" the interviewer asks. She is used to this. They have a fairly productive interview even though she is annoyed by the amount of gushing he is doing. Her grades, extracurriculars, and understanding of the company's various projects all receive toothy smiles and loud exclamations. He is also sure to mention he is both color blind and gender blind, something you wouldn't have to mention if you actually were color or gender blind. "Thanks Mary. HR will get back to you soon, I'm sure," he says. After the interview, as she walks out of the building, she realizes the only other Black person she has seen there is the male security guard. Mentally, she crosses this company off her list.

Okay. A lot happened. Let's unpack this experience.

Environmental microaggressions are physical cues. The pictures on the walls and the lack of a diverse workforce makes it clear to Marianne that she doesn't belong there. Despite the diversity cues on their online platform, the company is very white and male. Nonverbal cues are embedded in actions; the receptionist ignoring an interviewee, an action she would not take as the face of the organization if she cared about how Marianne would perceive it. She simply doesn't care about how it makes Marianne feel and doesn't instinctively see her as worthy of attention. Verbal microaggressions run the gamut from epithets such as "nigger" and "bitch" to the interviewer's express surprise at Marianne's achievements, him feeling the need to communicate that he would not be a biased assessor (a thinly veiled attempt to convince himself that he won't be biased), and possibly even surprised that Black people could have "white-sounding" names.

EXAMPLES OF MICROAGGRESSIONS AND WHAT THEY REALLY MEAN

Here is my attempt at explaining a few statements I have personally been told, heard from friends, or seen in pop culture. Again, these are personal deconstructions. Someone else might describe them differently, and that's fine.

- "I don't see race" and all other explicit invalidations of difference on the basis of race = Not everything is a race thing. I see you as a person, not a [insert race here] person, so let's keep that crazy jar closed.
- "This is not a gender thing" and all other invalidations of difference on the basis of gender identity = Women

have rights now. You need to calm down. The issue is some other thing.

- "You know that could have happened to anyone, right?" = Don't start on your bias thing. Anyone could have received that treatment. The world is fairer than you give it credit for.
- "Where are you really from?" = Obviously you are from some exotic country. Why else would you look the way you do?
- "Why do you sound white?" and all other shocked exclamations at your verbal communication skills = Well done you! Look at you overcoming.
- "You're pretty for a Black girl" = I did not know Black women could be pretty.
- "Let's ask what [insert your name here] thinks" = You are a representative of your people. Please educate me.
- Touching someone's person at all and especially without their permission = You are a curiosity that I have the right to handle.

The list above is not exhaustive. Themes emanating from microaggressive behavior include the following:

- Assumptions of intelligence
- Color blindness
- Alien in the space implying that you shouldn't be there
- Myth of meritocracy
- Pathologizing cultural values by expressing dominance of one kind of background and/or inferiority of another
- Sexual objectification
- Assumption of abnormality

• Denial of prejudiced experiences

RESPONDING TO MICROAGGRESSIONS: HOPPING THROUGH LANDMINES

When I complain to people, of all races and gender identities, I get a lot of advice. Some people ask, "Why didn't you do anything?" "Why didn't you say anything?" or the crown jewel, "Are you sure they meant it that way?" Such is the minefield of navigating life's experiences. Victims worry they might be blowing the situation out of proportion. You can be accused of having a victim mentality, by yourself and by others. Maybe we're too sensitive. Maybe this is one-sided. This rests on a societal assumption of minimal harm. This assumption can force the victim to do nothing. The action may not be worth it. This is for multiple reasons.

1. Attributional ambiguity—Did this really happen? Am I misunderstanding the situation? As a minority, you exist in a state of heightened vigilance, a hypersensitivity brought on by your reality. Maybe you are creating your anger and victimhood.

2. Response indecision—How am I meant to respond? The shock of recognizing an invalidation of your experience is disorienting. What do you say? What do you do? What will be perceived as reasonable?

3. Time-constraints—If the conversation or interaction has moved past the comment, it can feel difficult, even impossible to bring the microaggression up again. Has the opportunity to confront the perpetrator disappeared?

4. Denying your own experience and reality—Self-delusion; telling yourself it did not happen, they meant it in a complimentary way, the misunderstanding is on your part. Maybe you don't want to deal with the emotional labor. Maybe you don't want to recognize bias in someone you respect, care about, or need to interact with.
5. Impotency of actions—So I say something. Then what? Maybe they feel bad and say sorry. Most likely, they feel offended, and I get categorized as over-sensitive or difficult. I'd rather just keep it moving.
6. Fearing consequences—A massive factor at play is power differentials. This could be a student confronting a lecturer, an employee confronting their boss, or even just a couple of friends having a harmless chat. They said something unsavory to you because they could and the social or economic capital you might lose by forcing them to confront their actions simply is not worth it.

IMPACT OF MICROAGGRESSIONS

In many ways, the insidious nature of microaggressions exists in a clash of realities, seeing and experiencing the world in different ways. The dominance of one kind of experience requires that other groups assimilate, for example, women learn how to survive a male-dominated work culture, and those in the minority code switch. Any and all slights are perceived to cause minimal harm and so are things to move on from. This allows perpetrators to continue these toxic behavior patterns and imposes a mental and emotional load on victims. In his book

Microaggressions in Everyday Life, Derald Wing Sue provides the following effects of minimizing microaggressive behavior on victims:

- attack the mental health of victims by causing anger, frustration, low self-esteem, and emotional turmoil
- create a climate and culture of hostility and invalidation
- perpetuate stereotype threat, a phenomenon where people begin to conform to stereotypical ideas about their social groups
- negatively impact physical health
- lower productivity
- saturate society with signals about the lower value of certain groups

WHAT CAN YOU DO?

This is an incredibly difficult question to answer. First, I want to tell you that your feelings, whether they are anger or anguish or something in between, are valid. If someone made you feel some kind of way, their intention isn't the point, your feelings are. If you felt hurt, insulted, disrespected, or some other indescribable emotion, acknowledge that feeling. I hope that the people around you are supportive and validating. If they aren't, I am supporting and validating you from afar. You did not bring this upon yourself. It's shitty. I'm sorry.

A Harvard Business Review report provided the following framework for managing microaggressions. It goes as follows:

STEP 1: DISCERN

Is it worth responding?

I do not want to tell you to do nothing. What I do hope is that you make an empowered choice that feels as good as it could and works for you. Consider all the factors at play: relationship politics, emotional labor, and continued impact. Given all of this information, do you still want to confront them? You, not your friends or an official you are speaking to, yourself. Sadly, if there is an uneven power dynamic at play, you might see it as a waste or disadvantage to compromise your long-term prospects to engage. That's fine too. Do not feel bad for acting in a way that preserves your peace and your prospects. It's okay to recognize the fact that this might continue to hurt you and choose to avoid the pain.

STEP 2: DISARM

How can we stop the perpetrator from acting defensively?

People don't usually take well to being told they are biased. They will likely instinctively reject your concerns. I am sorry to say this, but you may need to communicate your problem in a palatable way, which allows it to remain cordial. Thankfully, 2020 brought on a racial reckoning that has allowed us to communicate more clearly and expect more empathy. Begin a dialogue and invite them to engage with you.

STEP 3: DEFY
Make yourself clear.

Challenge them to clarify their statement. Ask what they meant. Even if their intentions were not malicious, they need to understand their impact was. Even if they assert the innocuous nature of their comment, you must assert their unkind reality. Acknowledge their perspective but share your reality.

STEP 4: DECIDE
What does this moment mean to you? I believe your priority should be protecting your peace. Life should be joyous and enjoyable. Yes, in practice, it's imperfect and occasionally heartbreaking. Yes, there are uncomfortable and unfair moments too. But we do what we can to be happy. Do what you need to do to be at peace with this interaction. Do what you need to protect your mental health and well-being.

To allies, get comfortable with being uncomfortable. Understand that you don't know better and educate yourselves. Yes, members of minority groups have lived through experiences that could provide a positive learning opportunity for you. But remember, it is not their responsibility to teach you. It is not their job to rehash their pain for your benefit. Books, podcasts, movies, essays, YouTube videos, documentaries, and TV shows exist. They have rehashed these topics time and again. Find them and use them.

Allies, learn what a microaggression is and recognize them coming from yourself and others. If you didn't say something that could be categorized as biased, your tone and manner are important as well. How you say it carries as much weight and can cause as much pain. You have access to privileges that minorities do not. You are less likely to be penalized for highlighting a microaggression, demanding an acknowledgment and apology. Realize that your intention means less than their experience. Be open to hearing them out. Be fair and empathetic in order to have a dialogue. This is important so pay attention; microaggressions are unjust and they create a hostile and invalidating social experience that insults, demeans, and invalidates marginalized groups. Be a part of the solution.

To organizations, you have an ethical mandate to create inclusive spaces. Consider this a non-exhaustive list of questions. Do you have a policy in place? Does it have clear and fair disciplinary procedures? Is this clear to all members of your community? How do you continuously work to make spaces inclusive? How do you involve marginalized groups in decision-making and improving the social climate? How do you recruit and retain diverse talent? Do you have a diverse management team or board? Do you play a role in making society at large a supportive environment?

This chapter has been filled with a lot of information. Feel free to take a pause to digest it. Open up your phone or laptop and do the research you need to do. If you recognize your own experiences here, I'm so sorry that happened to you. If you recognize your previous actions here, apologize. An apology is not everything, but it is a first step.

BLACK WOMEN ON MICROAGGRESSIONS

It just goes past genuine curiosity, right? They need to emphasize how different you are.

Blessing

If I asked you to think of something sexist or racist, it would probably be a very overt display of sexism or racism. You might picture someone rolling down the window as they pass me by and shouting out the N-word. Or you might imagine me walking down the street and having my ass groped by a stranger. You might be like, "Yeah, that's racism, or that's sexism." But the reality is that the majority of sexism and racism that we see playing out is a lot more subtle than that. And that's what a microaggression is. It's everyday sexism, racism, any other -ism in a seemingly innocuous or unnoticeable way to a member of a dominant group, but death by one thousand cuts to the person on the receiving end. So, a really good example of a microaggression is people mispronouncing names that they know they're going to mispronounce but they don't have the decency to just ask how to pronounce it. So you know, I have walked into places and been called Daisy, Dossi, and people saying, "I'll just call you Abby because that's easier for me." That's racist. If my name was Sally and no one's gonna make a big deal out of pronouncing my name wrong. If my name was Sally with two S's, they might just say, "Hey, that's a really interesting spelling. Can I just check before I pronounce it?" But as soon as it's slightly weird, no one cares. They're just gonna guess or they're gonna make it awkward. Another microaggression could involve the only mom on your team who takes every Wednesday off to look after her kid because that's when her husband has to be in the office. She comes in on a Thursday, like she does every Thursday after she spent Wednesday on childcare duties. You ask her, "Did you have a nice day off?" No, she didn't have a day off. She had a day at her other job raising a small human. Parenting is not a day off. Your statement suggests that parenting isn't actual work. That's not inclusive.

Abadesi

I was out for dinner with some friends, and we were talking about how there are small nuances to everyday experiences only women experience. And you know, the guys were like, "Oh, really, what are you talking about?" Immediately afterward, the waiter came over and said, "By the way, this is a new dish. What did you think about it?" And he only listened to the opinions of the men. We girls chipped in, and he didn't express interest in our feedback. Once he left, the look on the men's faces said, "Oh, my God. It's true."

Sinead

In the workplace, people often ask, "Oh, you've got plaits, and they lay on your head. How did you do that?" Or, they say things like, "Oh, you changed your hair again?" These sorts of comments are not necessary. If you see a colleague who is not aware of their own bias, call them out. It's about having really open discussions and drawing a line. I think early on in my career, I was very scared to establish these boundaries. But as I've grown older and gotten more authority within my career, it's gotten easier to stand up for myself.

Yvonne

INTERLUDE:

SOMETIMES PEOPLE SURPRISE YOU

I was tormented.

To someone else this may seem small, but it is a shocking, dehumanizing thing to be denied personhood. Especially when a nice person is the culprit. I remember meeting her on campus. It was freezing in the classroom. Classes during COVID-19 meant air circulation, so all the windows in the fifth-floor room were wide open.

She was funny, and I remember thinking, "Thank God she's in my group. Working with her will make this project a lot easier." The next week, we all stayed home (hybrid learning meant a third of the class was freezing in person in a university building but logged into Zoom for the teaching. If this is a Zoom lesson, I can do it from my bedroom).

That was the first time it happened, the gaslighting. I was being spoken over and ignored. It is an incredibly disorienting experience to speak and have no one acknowledge it. Having your comment echoed by another person is upsetting, but what's truly a slap in the face is having everyone else applaud this "new" idea. I was losing my mind. It didn't just impact me during sessions or when I had to jump on a team call, I thought about this constantly.

Occasionally, the men in my group affirmed my personhood. They reminded people who tried to steal my ideas that I had already shared them. They spoke directly to me, drawing me to the center of the conversation, allowing me to contribute. I always expect better of white women. I assume the shared experience of womanhood and sexism will make them allies but, in this case, they were the active aggressors. Women know better. This girl knew better.

I decided I needed to confront her. I was emboldened by the events of 2020 to want a response. I wanted her to know what she had done and to know I knew the truth of what happened.

But then, I got scared.

Righteous anger is easy in the comfort of your bedroom, loud when you practice with yourself in the bathroom mirror but shockingly quiet when you face the person whose actions have harmed you. I found excuses. It was never a good time. I didn't want to ruin the team atmosphere (a comical idea given how toxic the environment already was for me). I didn't want her to turn against me (hadn't she already?). I didn't want to draw too much attention to it or me (they didn't need another moment to gaslight me). I was scared, so I held off. I decided to send her a message right after we submitted the project. I began drafting the message. I sent it to a friend for feedback, and she validated me. She said, "This has happened to me too. I am so sorry." A far cry from my boyfriend who asked if I was sure about what was happening.

We recorded the video for the final submission, said bye, and wished each other luck. Now was the moment I had been waiting for. But I had two exams to study for and she had one, so I didn't want the fallout of this confrontation to affect either of our revision periods. So, again, I held off. After the exam, for a moment, I decided not to send it. I was happy to have survived the semester and to finally be going home. I was happy and didn't want to go back to being unhappy. So, the days flew by, Christmas and New Year's, yet a part of me was not over it.

Could I move on? Sure, I could. She wasn't the first, and she won't be the last. But in a year, when the world realized we had to be anti-racist, I felt like I deserved more than moving on.

I sent this message:

Hi.

I felt the need to communicate something to you. In multiple consecutive meetings for our group project, you ignored my comments and spoke over me. You never did this to anyone else, and it happened multiple times so I can't ignore it and blame it on tech issues. It made me feel small and invisible. I reduced my contributions to discussions because 2020 was filled with too much Black trauma for me to increase my own. When we met on campus, I thought you were really nice, and I don't think you were intentionally silencing me.

But you were silencing me.

As a woman, I think you can appreciate what I mean. Being at this university, I am often the only Black person and Black woman. Simply existing is hard. I'm not trying to attack you. I just want you to be more aware and empathetic for the benefit of the next Black woman you work with.

I hope your exams went well and you had a lovely Christmas break. You are a really nice person, and you were an incredible person to have on the team xx.

Half an hour later, this was her reply.

Hi Lauryn,

I just want to start by saying how incredibly sorry I am. I'm so sorry that the way I acted on the team calls made you feel so horrible. I can't imagine how difficult this year has been for you, and I would never want to add to that pain. Your message is filled with so much kindness, and I'm also sorry that I've put you in a position where you had to message me.

I do know what you mean about being a woman in STEM, and I'm so sorry that I silenced you when others have done something similar to me. I know it must be harder for you, and I apologize for not giving you the space to speak. It's easy for me to say sorry but I do truly mean it. I also hope you had a lovely Christmas and wish you all the best for the upcoming semester xx.

I was lucky to get such a nice response. I am also aware that I very carefully curated my message. I made it kind, palatable, and nonthreatening to her sense of self. I did a lot of the work. But I did it. For the first time, I held a mirror to someone's face and made them aware of what they did. I'm proud of that.

CHAPTER 7

A NOTE TO ALLIES

In order to empathize with someone's experience you must be willing to believe them as they see it and not how you imagine their experience to be.

—BRENÉ BROWN

Firstly, thank you for picking up this book. Maybe it was an act of curiosity or maybe it was an active choice to learn about an experience separate from your own. Either way, I hope you are ready for some harsh truths. Privilege blinds us. And it's rarely an active or malicious act. Your experiences shelter you from some truths. I am an able-bodied, cisgender, heterosexual woman. These are layers of privilege. It took a lot of conversations and reading as well as being politely, and sometimes aggressively, called out for me to actively think about experiences separate from my own.

A couple of years ago, I was in charge of running the TEDx student speaking program. One participant attended the first session and none of the sessions after that. I had reached out a few times to ask about her absences and she always promised to come the next week. One week, after yet another no show, I contacted her to officially discharge her from the program. My message read, in part, "A minimum attendance is required if you wish to participate in the final showcase. I totally understand if university or your mental health is taking precedence at this time. I hope you understand why I have to let you go. Please do re-apply next semester." Now, I pride myself on being a decent person to work with. I actively practice empathy with my teammates and prioritize their mental well-being. When she replied to me, I realized my range of understanding needed to be better. "I am a disabled person," she began, "and you keep hosting sessions in rooms that are harder to get to for me."

I felt like an asshole. As one of those annoying "take the stairs for a healthy heart" people, I was not always aware of the presence of elevators or ramps and other accommodations that would be necessary for others. As someone who values inclusive thought and was eager to get started with the racially and experientially diverse set of female student speakers, I failed to create an inclusive space. I had failed as an ally. Even though she left the program, I began to think about room accessibility when I made bookings. My eyes had been opened to my privilege and I decided to do better.

This book will open your eyes to your privilege in relation to the experiences of Black women. And it is an icky, uncomfortable experience to realize that you are causing so much harm to others. It prompts feelings of guilt, anger, and embarrassment. Maybe you'll want to separate yourself from that feeling by exiting the conversation. Again, you are exercising your privilege. Black women cannot exit the conversation. Maybe you'll emphasize your past good deeds. Please stop. There is no prize for being only semi-problematic. Maybe you'll go silent because you're fearful of being attacked, canceled, or called out. Remember this:

Those who stand silent in the face of oppression stand with the oppressor.

—DESMOND TUTU

Here's what you should do.

1. Own your privilege
Recognize the fact that who you are, a literal cosmic accident, has provided you with resources and advantages, both social and economic. Really think about how your actions have left people around you, often people unlike you, feeling othered. Do some serious and honest reflection.

2. Apologize
Go and apologize. Send an email or text or smoke signal. Be specific about what you did, so it is clear you understand and repent for the harm you caused. General mea culpas are almost worse than not saying anything because they are asking for absolution for a harm that has not been carefully considered. Own your actions and recognize the impact of your actions. Don't do it for you. This is not your moment to feel better about yourself.

This is a time to allow another person to feel a bit better. Obviously, sorry doesn't solve all problems. Do not expect a reply. It's not their job to reply.

3. Talk about the uncomfortable
Essentially, when allowed privilege, we become complicit in oppressive systems. Do not read this book or any other book about the experiences of marginalized communities or individuals and then talk about their trauma as though you understand it. You can't ever understand it. What you can understand and speak on is the oppressive system and your role within it. What you can understand is how to be a part of the solution.

4. Do your research
There are books, podcasts, articles, documentaries, and a lot of resources out there. Please educate yourself. Ignorance causes harm.

5. Resist developing a savior complex
You cannot fly in and fix communities that aren't yours. Without knowing their needs, you cannot create the change they need. You will think you're doing exactly what they need and that will make you feel good about yourself. People and their pain do not exist to make you feel better about yourself. Such actions are often detrimental. Really think about what a positive contribution would be and involve the people who have the lived experiences to inform your actions.

6. Start with the people around you

Call out friends, family members, and co-workers. Your privilege insulates you from repercussions that another person may experience from defending themselves. People may also be more likely to listen and engage with the issue if it comes from a member of the in-group. This is a real opportunity to effect positive change.

7. Speak up but not over

As much as I encourage you to speak up, you must never speak over someone who has lived the experience. Do not co-opt their messages and frame them as your own. This conversation isn't about you. Feed into it, but never turn the spotlight onto yourself. Share your platforms. That's a wonderful way to amplify the messages that need to be shared.

8. What can you do?

Yes, joining the protests, sharing the links, liking the posts, supporting businesses and initiatives founded by, run by, and that support "othered" groups are very important actions. But also, really think about any position of power or influence you hold. Can you stand up to a bully? Can you amplify the voices of people on your teams at work or school? Can you share your advantages with another by teaching them skills you've accumulated? Can you invite people onto your team or advocate for them to be considered for recognition or a promotion? Can you collaborate with an initiative or charity, be it through financial support or providing other resources? An important thing we all need to do is believe people. Don't assume something couldn't happen just because you haven't personally experienced it. Listen and ask questions but never invalidate.

9. Push yourself

This will be uncomfortable and scary. Remember it is a lot less scary than the experiences of the oppressed. Commit to pushing past your fears and supporting impactful change.

10. Ally is a verb

The most important thing is that you remember to do the work. Allyship isn't just thinking well of people who aren't like you. It is doing what you can in your life to support the creation of a more equal society.

BLACK WOMEN TO ALLIES

It's so important that you're not speaking for Black women, or speaking over Black women, but giving them a space to tell their own stories.

Oyinda A.

The truth is, we can't achieve equality, we can't achieve equal opportunities, without equity, without leveling the playing field, without providing resources that will mitigate some of the challenges certain ethnic groups are going to face because of who they happen to be. I think for larger institutions, they definitely have a responsibility to think more sensitively as well. I think the assumption that, you know, Black people should just get over racism is so dangerous, particularly as a student. People are going to think this is what they have to tolerate.

Olamide

Inclusion to me means giving space and resources for everyone to have a voice and equitable opportunity to show and make a difference. As people of color, we don't just become champions of diversity and inclusion just because of our skin. Inclusion is an invitation to be enlightened, to offer opposing views without ridicule or retribution. As a thought leader, I want to shift how corporate, public, and private industry leaders see women of color and how we together can make space, make room, and collaborate so our collective needs are met—even the basic ones such as health, personal growth, being heard, and feeling protected and valued.

Karrin

Support would mean allowing me to stand up for myself. I don't want someone to speak for me unless I ask you to. It makes me feel silenced in a different way. I want you to stand beside me, not save me. If I take a step, say, "Yes, I'm with you. You're not alone in this fight while you're concentrating on the front and seeing what's happening. I will look left and right and see all the other things that might be coming at you."

Cecirahim

As an ally of women in STEM, I would advise that if you are already in STEM, mentor and take as many women with you as you grow, learn, and rise. If you are not, please work on helping more women and girls access the opportunities needed to help them understand these fields better, as we do for so many other careers.

Regina

Do not depend on students to do free labor for your diversity, equity, and inclusion initiatives. Do invest in people with expertise. Black people are not experts just because we're Black. Be mindful of the emotional labor and the burden it takes for people of color to do this work as well.

Jasmine

I'm weary of asking institutions to make changes. I don't think it'll be genuine. I think that they will have folks do stuff who ought not be doing stuff. And that can make interactions worse. Instead, what I think we really need is to have a conversation with each other. And what I mean by that is, there are so many times in academia, whether you're a student or you're faculty, that you look at stuff, and think, "These folks racist, right? They are sexist, right?" But then if you really take a step back, you realize they are just a mess. They're just awful. They do it to everybody. It feels different when you are a woman or Black because of everything else you carry. We put so much of the responsibility on institutions for change, without recognizing that we are the institutions. The institution isn't this big body. It's the individuals who work there. How many of us are modeling the change we want?

Rhonda

Because one of the things that we do, particularly as Black people, is that we continue to download our trauma,

time and time again to justify it and to convince someone else that what we're talking about is real. I've got to
debate with you whether it's even real before we can even
address what's happened to me. I can't keep download-
ing my trauma for you and sensationalizing it to induce
shock and horror. I don't have the energy for that. Here's
the bottom line. Whilst we might come at it from different perspectives and have different experiences, nobody
can say the world is not treating us (Black people) in a
way that is systemically unfair, for no other reason other
than the fact that we have darker skin. That's the core
of it. We can have lots of conversations about that. But
we know and whether that's health, policing, education,
corporate, in every facet of life, we're at the bottom. And
that's wrong.

Aisha

So first of all, in order to make it more inclusive for us,
they have to recognize they have white privilege. That's
the first really difficult thing because people don't want
to give up their privilege. If you call yourself an ally, you
give up your privilege and help Black and BIPOC people
succeed. You know, we can tell you to read all the books,
right? But if you ain't taking the action, it's pointless.
Understand what you can do to stop the next person of
color from being pushed out of the department, use your
privilege to protect the Black Student department or say
we need more Black and brown people in these depart-
ments. Don't be silent. Talk about these issues, bring it
to the forefront and say, "This isn't right." That's just
the start.

Ashley

To be patient, to listen, to be open-minded. It's not going to be easy to be an ally at first because people are angry with the social injustice that happened in 2020 and throughout history. A lot of people are angry, and we want allies, but we want people who are consistent. So allyship requires consistency and commitment.

Malika

We should be paying people to work on equity and diversity in schools and universities. At my institution, it's on a volunteer basis and that isn't good enough. It makes a clear statement about what we think about the issue in general if we won't pay people to do it, right? How do we hold people accountable when it's not their main job? People are rightfully busy with teaching and research. The key thing is getting qualified people working on these questions and creating the right solutions. We should invest in it because it is an important task for the department.

Estifa'a

A really prominent psychologist in the open science space appropriated a Martin Luther King quote about open science and transparency on Twitter. And honestly, I could see why he thought it was a clever play on words and wanted to use it. But then somebody pointed out to him that it wasn't quite right for him to take on this quote that was really about racial injustice and use it the way he did. He just dug his heels in and said, "Don't project your views onto me." I had quite a few offline conversations where people were outraged, but he continued to be impervious to the criticism. What he could have done was say, "I wrote this with good intention but upon reflection on what you're saying, I can see why it's not quite right." But he didn't do that. This is a man with power and influence. I didn't feel able to call him out. But white allies were able to say, "This is why people of color don't feel welcome in this space. They tell you what you're saying is not right, but you dismiss it. It's not for somebody not affected by these issues, to tell people who are affected by these issues, that this is not important or a problem." That is the role of allies. They have the ability to stand up with less risk.

Emily

For allies to actually be effective, they need to be able to listen and understand the stories and the experiences of the people they aim to support. It's about understanding exactly what the pain point of those people is and then, it's your responsibility to be able to help drive that change.

Blessing

Allies need to continue engaging with marginalized or minority communities to go beyond what they see on social media and the need to be woke. Even though we are a minority group, we are not homogeneous. The experience of one person doesn't necessarily apply to all of us just because we share an identifying characteristic.

Allies shouldn't get caught up in the commonalities of us as a minority and try to apply the same situations and solutions to all of us. We are still individuals, and the different sides of the story need to be told and heard to implement better solutions.

Busola

I've been challenged on my assumptions so much, and I love it; bring it on. No human knows everything. I want to be challenged, and I want to make sure someone else's experience is better. It blows my mind that people can't experience uncomfortability for one second just to understand the struggle someone goes through for their whole entire life.

Allies need to let go of their egos. The world is not good or bad. And the fear of being seen as bad grips our whole being. As if being called out means we're unworthy of everything. That's not true. We all need to be empathetic and open to being wrong.

Bola

Allies. You can't be pro-diversity at work and an asshole to women and minorities once you leave the office. Which is the truth? If you accept me, you need to support me. Stand up for me, not out of pity but respect. You have more leverage, and you should use it.

Hajer

Educate yourself. That's more than saying, "Oh, I know about this system of oppression." It's saying, "I understand how I fit into that system of oppression." Self-reflection is the biggest thing you can do in terms of figuring out how you behave and how that might impact people around you.

Danielle

One of the things that perpetuates a lack of diversity in tech is a lack of understanding of systemic oppression, individual bias, and the way systems of oppression and lack of awareness of our own biases perpetuate the status quo. Either you're taking action and challenging the status quo or you're doing nothing and thus supporting and perpetuating it. We're fighting against centuries, if not millennia of superiority and inferiority and stereotypes. Inaction is worse than action that doesn't hit the mark. As a company, institution, or anyone with power, it's better to show what you tried, even if you failed, than to just not try. That is a recurring theme because there are a lot of people who are still just talking. Now is the time for action and the willingness to take risks.

Abadesi

PART 3

THE EARLY YEARS

INTERLUDE:

DOCTOR, LAWYER, ENGINEER

These are the career options offered by African parents: doctor, lawyer, engineer, or disappointment.

Luckily, my parents are both accountants and spared me this messaging. They asked me to try my best in school. What they meant was "come first." And I tried my best to meet this expectation. I knew (read this as hoped) they would love me regardless, but I tried my hardest to at least make the top three.

Now, I am incredibly grateful for this push early on. I wasn't necessarily ambitious or competitive and might not have tried as hard of my own volition. Now, I am a hard worker and a smart planner because I have gotten a lot of practice doing those things. The resilience I developed studying at 4 a.m. before classes, bouncing back from loads of rejections and unkind feedback from kind and unkind teachers continues to serve my development.

It is very important to acknowledge the importance of parents and guardians and how they can impact your educational choices and interests. The conditioning I received at home to strive for excellence, alongside the private education my parents invested in, gave me options; at the end of high school, I got all A*s (an A* is a grade above 90 percent) and could decide to do anything.

My father would have preferred it if I had become an accountant as well. I remember him begging me to take accounting when I wanted to do additional maths. We sat with the school form between us, debating options for at least forty-five minutes. I say debate but what I mean is I had a set list of what I wanted to do, he had a set list of what he wanted me to do, and we exchanged pleasantries until someone gave in. Luckily, I outlasted him and pursued the science pathway, even though a part of me is still sad I never got to study English literature. I was going to be a hematologist because my siblings have sickle-cell anemia and watching them be continuously ill broke my heart. Like every fledgling doctor, I thought I might figure out how to cure them. Sadly, I found biology incredibly boring, so I had to change my plans. Then, I decided I wanted to be an actuary. I don't know who convinced a fourteen-year-old girl that the insurance industry was the dream, but it became my dream.

When I progressed to A levels (a required pre-university qualification in the United Kingdom and offered internationally) and announced to my parents that I would be taking mathematics, business, economics, and global perspectives and research, my father was not impressed.

He remembered how determined I was to stay on a science track and was impossibly annoyed I didn't just listen to him in the first place. My father is not too big of a man to say, "I told you so." I chose not to argue my case. It's always best to pick your battles when dealing with your parents, and I began looking at actuarial science degree programs.

My parents really liked this idea and readily shared my plans with their friends. I remember being a month into A levels, university was still at least a year and a half away, and I would meet friends of my parents who would say I was a smart girl to choose to be an actuary because they are so few in Zambia and I would make good money. Perfect strangers cosigning a plan that I had yet to put in motion. Teachers loved the idea too and my overactive imagination began to fantasize about what my life would look like as an actuary. I couldn't find too much about the day-to-day online, so I drew a bland, deskbound picture. But having something to work toward, which people found compelling, was incredibly motivating during long hot days of studying.

The autonomy I have enjoyed over my academic choices is incredibly rare, and I am privileged in that way. My parents respected that I knew myself and supported my education, not always without complaint but always with pride. I gained a full scholarship from the MasterCard foundation to pursue my undergraduate degree at the University of Edinburgh and the team there gave me the freedom to pursue whatever academic path I wanted. I actually enrolled as a maths and business student because the lack of STEM-related support from adults in my life worried me into half-committing to a course they claimed would assure me a job post-graduation. I barely attended one lecture before I decided to swap business for economics. At the end of my second year, I gave up the economics and focused myself on just the maths. I knew what I wanted to do, but because I was so scared of making the wrong choice, I tried things. We ask young people to decide on life paths at eighteen and the implied finality of this choice is terrifying. It's one of the first adult choices I was asked to make, and it was incredibly daunting.

In the spirit of becoming an actuary, I pursued my maths degree. With time, my plans have changed. I no longer want to be an actuary. I enjoy maths for maths' sake. I enjoy it because it challenges me, it allows for a lot of creativity, and the *aha* moment you get when you figure something out is the best reward.

Now, I have gotten a lot of unsolicited feedback about my choice of degree. Uncles calling it useless and unemployable, friends incredulous as to why I would punish myself in this way, and old teachers doubting I could manage it. Luckily, I'm stubborn.

CHAPTER 8

TEACHERS, ANXIETY TRANSFER, AND STEREOTYPE THREAT

Math anxiety is a common thing.

A lot of people will tell you, loudly, that they aren't any good at math. As a maths undergrad, I was constantly bombarded with comments from *everyone*. Border control officials making small talk, family members, and other students would have their mouths hanging in aghast at my news. They could not imagine putting themselves through the trauma of a degree of mathematics (I for one could not imagine putting myself through the trauma of an engineering degree, but different strokes I guess). What did I find particularly interesting? Their insistence that I was either brilliant or crazy. Their perception of maths and its accelerating difficulty allowed them to construct certain beliefs about it. They saw it as impossible, and so, intentionally or unintentionally, they wanted me to see it as impossible too.

Anxiety transfer. This happens when you share your fears about something with someone else who then begins to share them. In part, I did buy into everyone's fears. It exacerbated my imposter syndrome each time I was reminded that I must either be crazy or inhuman. I might have changed to something else. I would have made a significant shift based on the anxiety transfer from the people around me. Fortunately, I stuck with my plan. We can't assume that level of self-determination or stubbornness in children. That makes them a lot more vulnerable to anxiety transfer.

Anxiety is a very personal feeling, but it can, and often does, have external triggers. It is a protective reflex based on cues we have been exposed to. There are multiple sources of this anxiety. It could be a learned anxiety based off cues from adults or media. It could be an internalized anxiety from poor historic performance that yielded poor feedback. A study was carried out by Maastricht University in the Netherlands on second and fourth grade children (Van Miller et al, 2019). They found that maths anxiety significantly and negatively impacted the young girls in the study, especially the second-grade girls. This accounts for the impact of test anxiety as well. Explicitly, young girls who think maths is hard and go on to score poorly in math tests.

Where do we get inspiration for our aspirations? We get them from our toys, the TV, our parents, the role models in our life, and the fun things in our orbits.

For years, I wanted to be a teacher. I thought my teachers were superstars, and I wanted to be like them. Of course, as time went on, I realized I wasn't well-suited to teaching. I got a lot of positive feedback from my English teachers. I loved to read, and it made me a solid creative storyteller. And based on their feedback, I wanted to be a full-time author. At other points, I have wanted to be a hematologist, astrophysicist, news anchor, businesswoman, and fashion designer. Dreams are fluid things for some of us. I have friends who have wanted to be doctors for as long as I have known them and never wavered. Their dreams and aspirations have always been clear to them.

All kinds of things and people have an impact on our dreams. Parents and guardians, particularly those from African backgrounds, can dictate certain dreams to you. Teachers, who are the gatekeepers of knowledge, can persuade or dissuade you to see a future in certain areas of inquiry. Little kids are taught to be self-conscious. They are taught doubt. By themselves, they would just dream. Sadly, societal constraints don't allow for every dream.

There was an enormous body of masculine opinion to the effect that nothing could be expected of women intellectually. Even if her father did not read out loud these opinions, any girl could read them for herself; and the reading, even in the nineteenth century, must have lowered her vitality, and told profoundly upon her work. There would always have been that assertion— you cannot do this, you are incapable of doing that—to protest against, to overcome.

—VIRGINIA WOOLF (A ROOM OF ONE'S OWN)

Girls are bad at math. We hear this constantly, and it can become internalized. Some people would ask women and girls to brush this aside. It's a comment made by small-minded people. We should pay them no mind and so on. But words have power. Spencer, Steele, and Quinn carried out a study in the late 1990s (Spencer et al, 1999). They assembled two groups of college students of equal ability levels to participate in an experiment. They were given a maths test. One group was told that the experiment was being done to explore gender differences in maths ability and the other group was given a neutral reason for the assessment. What emerged is incredibly telling. In the control group, there were limited gender differences in attainment. However, for the group exposed to the explicit threat of negatively representing their gender, there were significant differences in attainment, as much as a twenty-point difference in scores.

The phenomenon I am describing is called stereotype threat. Stereotype threat is a situation in which people are or feel themselves to be at great risk of conforming to stereotypes about their social group (Steele, 1997). Being reminded that girls are bad at math causes anxiety, which negatively impacts their performance. One theory brought forward to explain this uses the concept of working memory (Beilock, Rydell & McConnell 2007). Participants are dedicating a significant amount of their working memory to negative thoughts like "Can I really do this?" "What makes me so special?" and "They clearly don't expect much of me...maybe they're right not to." We have activated concerns about ability. I'm sure you can empathize with this feeling. I've sat through countless exams where my distress has blocked all practical thoughts. I occasionally have taken a minute to have a quick panic before continuing. No one wants to be a failure. And besides these unproductive thoughts, there are physical manifestations of this anxiety such as increased heart rate and nervous sweats. This results in physical and mental fatigue, which reduces your capacity to engage with the task at hand.

Unsurprisingly, another study showed that when African American students were told that a verbal assessment was being used to assess ability, their performance was negatively affected (Steele & Aronson 1995). When it was described as a simple lab task, their performance matched that of equally skilled white participants. Racial stereotypes about intellectual ability provided an opportunity for stereotype threat.

And for a Black woman, there exists double jeopardy.

For stereotype threat to occur, three factors must be present. Firstly, you need to have a conscious or unconscious knowledge of the stereotype being implied. Otherwise, you wouldn't be threatened. Secondly, you need to have a strong connection with the stereotyped group. If you do not perceive yourself to be a member of the group or identify with that membership status, you are less concerned about whether you represent it well. Finally, you need to be concerned about the domain of reference. So, as a Black woman in STEM who is acutely aware of the lack of representation and your role as a golden stereotype-defying representative, stereotype threat is especially strong.

Interestingly, another study found that when women participated in a maths diagnostic assessment under an alias, they performed better (Zhang, Schmader & Hall 2013). Their reputation was safe from being associated with the negative stereotype. They no longer had to worry about being seen as an example of a harmful stereotype and could concentrate on the task at hand. I cannot condense the entirety of psychological enquiry in this chapter. What I can say is, evidently, it's not a question of ability. It is one of anxiety, unfairness, and prejudice.

Let me theorize something. Suppose you're seven years old again. You love school because you love seeing your friends and you get to learn new things. Your teacher does something interesting. When you, a little Black girl, doesn't score very well on a mental maths test, they comfort you by saying, "Don't worry too much. Girls aren't very good at maths. Let's work a bit harder at it." When Ben doesn't score very well, they say, "You just need to work a little harder." Did you notice something? This little girl now implicitly understands that people like her don't do well. The task of improvement, though not impossible, is described as bigger than her. Maybe you are shaking your head. A teacher would never say something like this. But I need you to pause and think about it. I have a distinct memory of my maths teacher telling me that maths for girls "can be hard." I was eighteen and telling him about my university applications. I was also his best student.

A 2015 Israeli study considered two sets of teachers (Lavy & Sand 2015). One group was given tests to grade, which had the names of the students on them, and the other group was given anonymized scripts. The named scripts yielded higher scores for boys while the anonymized ones yielded higher scores for girls. An anti-Pygmalion effect might be at play. Elementary or primary school teachers are statistically more likely to be female. According to a 2010 study, female math teachers who have high math anxiety negatively impact their female students, not their male students. As children growing into our gender identities, we model behaviors we see as gender-typical (Perry & Bussey 1979). Anxiety transfer is occurring, and biased teachers are grading with their biases in mind.

My teachers who opened up the universe to me also made sure to remind me how much of that universe I was allowed to call mine. I don't think they were being malicious. They were simply parroting beliefs and ideas that had been internalized and reinforced by the world they saw and lived in. And these comments, I hope, were in good faith. Whether conscious or unconscious, they were scared for me. That doesn't make them any less insidious or even malicious. They burdened me and made an uphill battle even more difficult.

BLACK WOMEN ON STEREOTYPES AND EXPECTATIONS

Being stereotyped as the sassy Black girl when I literally didn't even say anything and being seen as the person who's going to fight or the person who's going to beat someone up even when I've never shown any signs of aggression. It was hard.

Oyinda A.

I remember that my uncle once said, "Don't you think that you should encourage her to study something else instead of computers? Because if I found it hard, and I'm a man, how will she cope?" My mother was livid. She had an hour-long shouting match with him. And she basically said, "Please don't ever speak to my children like that. I don't allow that type of talk." In Zambia, the cut-off point for national examinations is different for boys and girls. It's much lower for girls and this is a deliberate government initiative done in order to encourage more girls to stay in school. On the surface, it sounds like a fantastic idea. It sounds like a fantastic policy. But I have an issue because of the quality of the girls who end up going to college. And I really don't like the fact that we have to downgrade the standards for girls. It's like saying, "They're never going to pass anyway; just give them a free certificate." And that is wrong.

Regina

So in upstate New York, where I studied, there are several prisons. Students come and go and, in the summer, it's a ghost town. So when I would walk around, people kept asking how I was, how my recovery was going, and I couldn't figure out why. They all thought I was just coming out of the prison system because that represented the experiences they had with Black people in that community.

Karrin

We need to start packaging the benefits for women and girls to help them understand why it is important for them to be in the STEM space; the career prospects but also the opportunity to play a part in changing how we live, work, and engage with ideas that might change the world.

Mbali

People talk about breaking the glass ceiling. I feel like the intersectionality of being a Black woman requires you to break a ceiling that's even higher than the normally defined one people are referring to. Intersectionality breaks that additional layer of gatekeeping because we are Black. When I see a Black woman do something, for me it carries greater weight. That's not to say that I don't appreciate the achievements of non-Black women. I just enjoy the representation of someone who looks like me. I definitely see that as a big deal. It's an added layer for me of defiance.

Cecirahim

They didn't tell me that I was going into a white, male-dominated field. That was something I had to learn on my own. And I would also say that you also learn on your own that there's a double standard and the rules are different and that you have to work twice as hard and that you're going to be working for people who are less qualified than you that tell you that you are not qualified. So those little things aren't taught in college, you just have to learn along the way.

Angela

So I say to my students, you've got a father and a son who go for a drive and, unfortunately, they are in an accident and then they get to the hospital. When they get there, the surgeon says, "I can't operate, that's my son." And then, I ask the students, how can that be? In a class that is all female, only 10 percent of the girls thought the doctor was his mother. They came up with all of the things you could possibly think of: grandad, same-sex relationship, stepdad. I had one girl argue with me and say the mom cheated and that was his biological father. And I thought, "You will picture the mom having an affair before you consider that a woman might be a doctor." The obvious reality, that they're well aware of, is that women can be surgeons. But, in that split second, unconscious bias takes over.

Aisha

Whenever you go to an interview, you'd be asked, "Would you be capable of leading a male team?" And then I'd think, come on, this is not about leading a male team, we are talking about leadership. I don't think leadership has a gender. You need soft skills which enable you to lead people to success.

Alda

I remember when we were forming the BlackEd movement (a student-led advocacy organization). We were very wary about coming out as angry Black women. It is a constant challenge we face whenever we have meetings. We always feel the need to not talk too much and not raise our voices. Even though we are being taken seriously, we are not taken as seriously as we should be.

Tumi

In our African countries, research or getting a PhD is not really taken seriously. You have to be a doctor, lawyer, accountant. I asked myself if I really wanted to be a doctor. I'm still figuring out if it came from me or if it's me absorbing the narrative around me. When I traveled, I realized that research was interesting to me. I could make discoveries. I realized life is not limited to certain things and I could become many things.

Tombi

In the UK, the systems can be so discouraging toward Black children. It comes up when you go to career advice meetings at school. The first thing they always advise young Black kids to do is to get into the music industry, and they ask them, "Would you like to be a rapper?" So, from the very beginning, STEM is not presented as an option. Saying you can be an engineer. Yes, you can be an astronaut. And yes, you can be a prime minister. Those are not presented to young Black kids. And that's the narrative that we really do need to change.

Sadiqah

The reason why I didn't like computer science in high school was that we started programming classes in the third and final year. And, I hated it because it wasn't taught very well. And so, I couldn't really take the information in the right way. And I didn't do well, and I hated it. It's really sad. All these kids hate math because they're not being taught math the right way. So, they're not good at it, and then they hate it and think they're crap. And we have this really bad feedback loop.

Hajer

If anything, my school experience was a battleground of illustrating to teachers that I was actually better than they thought I was. I even began to leave my name off my work because it would make my marks higher.

Sinead

INTERLUDE:

THE SHURI EFFECT: WHAT SHURI MEANS TO ME

In February 2018, *Black Panther* came out. I am a proud Marvel superfan and had been eagerly awaiting this film ever since it was announced at Comic-Con in October 2014 and ever more impatiently after we met Chadwick Boseman's strong, honorable Prince T'Challa in *Captain America: Civil War.*

It was a Black superhero from the best in superhero content (fact, not opinion). It was going to be culture-defining, and I was beyond excited. My friends and I made a pretty big deal of this moment. We created a group chat to plan our expedition to the movie theater. You would think that making a booking on the cinema's website would be a throwaway task for a group of undergraduates, many of whom were pursuing STEM degrees, but alas, it took a lot of diplomacy, a few *Black Panther*-themed gifs and one or two squabbles. Our conversation was filled with good-natured banter as we argued about dates, times, and seating arrangements all while making jabs at each other's egos and busy social lives as we fought to reconcile everyone's schedules.

I can't lie. I was about to leave the messiness and watch the movie by myself. This was a film that deserved to be seen on premiere night. Besides, there is only so long you can avoid spoilers on social media, YouTube, and quite frankly, the news, given how big of a cultural moment this was.

Finally, we had a date, a time, tickets, and a plan. We were going to meet up beforehand, have a potluck and go to the cinema together. Now, we took this *very* seriously. Social media was flooded with pictures and videos from similar *Black Panther* events. People dancing as they walked out of the theaters, all dressed up in stunning traditional African fabrics, embodying the magic they had just seen on the screen. We took inspiration and took it a slight step further by painting our faces.

Finally, we were sitting in the dark theater. The usual ads played, and I was bursting. The moment had come, and we were going to watch it in 5G (if you haven't seen a Marvel film in 5G, change your life).

Everything about the film was stunning: the visuals, the banter, the magical realism, action sequences, and Wakanda, in its technologically enhanced, distinctly African glory. Wakanda is an amalgamation of the beauty of so many African nations and cultures, presented with respect and pride. The buzzing market streets, Nakia's bantu knots and even Kilmonger's tongue-in-cheek "Auntie." It looked like home and for that fact alone, it's a vital movie.

Now, onto the most important part. Shuri, the crown princess of Wakanda and their resident national chief technology officer, is a scene-stealer. She is brilliant, funny, and confident. She mocks her brother for his taste in shoes and his inability to understand the need to update his kimoyo beads. Marvel superheroes are known for the high-tech costumes and gadgets, and T'Challa made quite an impressive splash in *Captain America: Civil War*. Then we see the *Black Panther* jet, EMP discs and, of course, the Wakanda cloak that keeps the country and its secrets hidden. All of this and more, which I'm sure we are yet to see on screen, created by Shuri. The brilliant mind behind this incredible country is a sixteen-year-old girl.

Shuri's existence is equal parts surprising and obvious.

1. We have seen countless portrayals of child prodigies in media. She is just one addition to that list. Sheldon Cooper, Dexter, Wade from *Kim Possible*, Artemis Fowl, Stewie Griffin from *Family Guy*, Matilda, and so on. You know a lot of these. How many do you know who are Black? How many are Black and female? Exactly! Shuri surprises you because she's an anomaly. Yet, there is absolutely no reason why in fiction, Black girls can't be prodigies.

2. As an African, with African parents who has lived in that context, Shuri running things is genuinely perplexing. The fact that she is allowed so much power

and responsibility... I could not dream that up. The unique nature of African patriarchy as well as age-ism, racism, and sexism more generally does not create many opportunities for young Black women in decision-making and innovation. They are not supported, funded, or acknowledged when they manage to survive the hurdles and create something of value. Shuri being the boss is the fantasy countless little girls didn't even know they could have.

3. *Black Panther* is a film filled with empowered women, and they are framed as such. They support the film's core character with their own distinct skills and have space to share their points of view. Shuri is the king's baby sister. She could have been framed all manner of ways; maybe as a classical Disney princess or one of those vapid sitcom eldest daughters. Instead, she is an equal to T'Challa. They share a classic sibling dynamic and beyond that, he respects her expertise. Shuri joins the strong Okoye and Nakia as one of many phenomenal women in the Wakandan narrative. She represents one of many ways someone can contribute to a fight for the good.

Kids are very perceptive and infinitely creative. I'm sure you've found them playing astronauts, doctors, and all kinds of things. You're very likely to find little girls playing mommy with their plastic dolls. This book is about a lot of things, one of these is the power of seeing yourself in all spaces. Role models play a vital role in inspiring people, especially very young people. Shuri by being herself gives little girls, especially Black girls, something to look to and believe in. Because of her, more little Black girls will play scientist, inventor, and Shuri from *Black Panther*. This representation will create generations of young Black women in STEM, and it was fitting that I name my first book after a character who changed the way I saw the world.

CHAPTER 9

THE SCULLY EFFECT AND THE IMPACT OF ROLE MODELS IN MEDIA

I have never watched a single episode of the *X Files*. As it is a touchstone of pop culture, I have seen memes and clips. Being a big Gillian Anderson fan, I read a little on her *X Files* character, Dana Scully. She sounds incredible. A medical doctor and FBI agent who was the skeptic to Fox Mulder's believer in mysticism. People listened to her because she was competent. She is career driven yet human, courageous and extremely witty, rational and graceful. She's a role model for the ages. This portrayal gave rise to the Scully effect: more and more young women pursuing careers in science, medicine, and law enforcement with a perceptible increase in the number of women in these fields. According to research carried out by the Geena Davis Institute on Gender in Media, 63 percent of women who work in STEM say Dana Scully served as their role model, and a further 63 percent say Scully increased their confidence in excelling in a male-dominated profession.

Why would a TV character have such an impact? The media we consume can have both positive and negative effects. One such effect is the role model effect. The role model effect supports the growth and development of individuals in their personal and professional lives as a result of consuming images and stories of relatable individuals who make success seem attainable. Stereotypes can be dangerous because they can grossly simplify and misrepresent our world. Stereotypes like "nerds are inherently antisocial and awkward" breed false truths about STEM spaces, which discourage individuals who do not identify with the stereotypes. Young Black women may find it difficult to find STEM role models because the current gap implies scarcity. This is especially true in developing African countries with widespread populations across the rural-urban spectrum. Information can be scarce in the absence of privilege, so media representations could be the only way to learn about and see certain experiences.

Now, think about all the brilliant protagonists you have encountered in books, movies, and TV shows. How many are Black? How many are female? How many are female and Black? We are doing everyone a monstrous disservice by not showing diversity on the screen. I love Sherlock Holmes, Hermione Granger, Dr. Gregory House, Lisa Simpson, Sheldon Cooper, and Veronica Mars. But where is the Black prodigy on primetime? Where is our Dana Scully?

Below is a list of fictional characters who inspire me, and I hope they inspire you.

DOC MCSTUFFINS

Dottie "Doc" McStuffins is a seven-year-old with a magical stethoscope that allows her to talk to her toys. She wants to be a doctor, like her pediatrician mother and prepares for her future by treating her toys and dolls of various ailments. When confused, she asks her mother or grandmother for advice. Doc is a joyful personality with a big heart and a curious mind, and each episode sees her learning about how to care for others. She is absolutely adorable in her lab coat, polka dot leggings, and pink sneakers. Doc was also inspired by a real-life person, Dr. Myiesha Taylor, an emergency medicine physician who co-founded the Artemis Medical Society, an organization that nurtures women physicians of color in order to increase the physician workforce diversity and diminish healthcare disparities. Disney Junior named Doc's mother Myiesha in her honor.

MIRANDA BAILEY FROM *GREY'S ANATOMY*

Grey Sloan Memorial hospital would be nowhere without the tough love and brilliance of this woman. She is a wonderful teacher, a brilliant doctor, and has some of the best lines on the show. In the world of Shondaland, she has been allowed to be complex, brilliant, and emotional in ways that make her a great boss and well-rounded person. She apologizes when she makes mistakes and forcefully puts herself forward because people don't always expect brilliance when it comes in a package like hers. Across the many seasons, she trains interns, manages hospital politics, and engages in trailblazing research while balancing marriage and motherhood. Her struggles with obsessive-compulsive disorder provide a kind representation of Black women managing mental illness. She is proud of the work she does and would make a great inspiration for anyone interested in the world of medicine.

SHURI FROM MARVEL

Shuri was one of many standout characters in Marvel's *Black Panther*. She was, simply put, a brilliant mind who tinkers with tech and showcases her talents. She is creating the future but not in the mad scientist way we are used to. Beyond this, she was allowed to be her own person, a youthful vibrant personality with a great sense of humor. Young geniuses can often be portrayed as adults trapped in a kid's body with monotonous voices and a vague disdain for fun. Shuri got to roast her brother and change her country. She wasn't just a sidekick to her brother but a superhero in her own right and played a pivotal role not only in the narrative of this film but also *Avengers: Infinity War*, a consequential part of the overarching Marvel Cinematic Universe. As a character in canon, there are multiple comic book issues we can read as we wait to see her next on-screen appearance.

RAMSEY FROM *FAST AND FURIOUS*

The *Fast and Furious* franchise is unending. The stunts alone are jaw-dropping. Megan Ramsey is a hacker with the self-assured cockiness that tells you she is very good at what she does. She gets to be brilliant, headstrong, and beautiful. I would be remiss to ignore the fact that films, especially action films, tend to cast supermodels as geniuses to create a buffer of sensuality to their brilliance. That is incredibly annoying in a very misogynistic way. That being said, there is no reason why a girl who looks like Nathalie Emmanuel can't also create an elite hacking tool and carry herself with a confidence that only comes with knowing your shit.

AKEELAH ANDERSON FROM *AKEELAH AND THE BEE*

Akeelah and the Bee was a staple in my household. My mum loved the movie, and we all eventually learned the lines. Akeelah is a gifted speller. She studies endlessly and overcomes her imposter syndrome and parental pushback to win the national spelling bee. It explores themes such as race, class, community, the educational system, self-esteem, friendship, and empowerment. The film's writer-director Doug Atchison put it best when he said, "It's about this girl's insecurity about doing a thing that she hasn't seen people who look like her doing." Akeelah's relationship with her mentor, Dr. Larabee, is the role model effect personified. This man from her neighborhood made it, and she begins to think she can too.

MEG MURRY FROM *A WRINKLE IN TIME*

Meg is a curious, precocious girl who excels at science and maths. However, she has a low opinion of herself and believes she is dumb and ugly and this manifests in her behavior with teachers calling her "belligerent and uncooperative." She has the ability to achieve complex tasks, but she doesn't try. It's hard to be a young girl growing up in a world that doesn't like women. A world that places a premium on female beauty and not much else. A world that can be full of bullies. Meg is our hero. She saves her father from a conformist regime using her unique talents and powers because she is powerful exactly as she is.

This list should be much, much longer.

I raced through African folklore from various countries and cultures in search of role models to share in this chapter. Sadly, I didn't find any stories that focused on a girl or woman's talents that didn't center on marriage or the pursuit of marriage, beauty, or lack thereof; female ingenuity is always a result of jealousy. Research from Yale University exploring African folklore from Francophone Sub-Saharan Africa concluded that the stories and proverbs were misogynistic and majorly portrayed women negatively. If you know of the illusive story I seek, please share it.

Black female excellence, like achievement more generally, exists in multitudes and should be represented as such. We should be allowed complexity, imperfection, and the right to simply exist in books and movies and all the sources that often inspire dreams.

Let me leave you with an interesting piece of research. Dr. Emma Riley carried out an experiment to understand the impact of role models on secondary school exam performance in Uganda. She had two groups of students who were about to write exams, one watching the treatment movie, the other being a control group. She chose Queen of Katwe, the true story of Phiona Mutesi, a Ugandan chess player. Mutesi's story is one of adversity and chasing your dreams. She studies hard to learn how to read and write in order to get into a good school that will nurture her talent with chess. As a role model, she exhibits many positive traits. She has a growth mindset, she sets and achieves long-term goals through small, incremental steps, she understands that her lack of knowledge comes from lack of education and not inherent stupidity, and she shapes her own life. Seeing the movie improved exam performance with girls' scores increasing more and increasing the likelihood that they would stay in education. This story, set in their home country, about someone who looked like them, had an impact.

INTERLUDE:

BLACK WOMEN ON ROLE MODELS

You have to see role models; you have to see people who look like you. You can't be what you don't see. Even for myself, when I look at the next phase of my career, I don't see very many Black female CIOs (chief information officers). So, it seems a little unattainable. Seeing that representation helps you envision yourself in that person's shoes at a later stage.

Angela

My mentor really changed my life. She supported my journey into medicine. I saw so much of myself in her. She grew up in the same town as me and went to the same sixth form college. Her teachers discouraged her as well, but she pushed through it. I love seeing the woman she is now, practicing medicine, being a mother, and juggling all of these hats effortlessly. She spoke so much life into me, even when I didn't believe in myself and didn't think that I could do it.

Olamide

It struck me like a lightning bolt, striking the top of my head and went straight through my body. I'm from Suffolk, Virginia, so NASA, where *Hidden Figures* happens, is where my first job was. When I watched the movie, I recognized the buildings. I had worked there and had no idea about these incredible women. I was a Black girl in the very same place, and even I didn't know. It forever changed me. And it made me walk so much taller. When I think about giving up or when I get down on myself, that's what I think about.

Karrin

Julianne Malveaux, an economist, was probably the first Black woman who I saw and thought, "Oh, this is a Black woman. She's out here doing her thing. She's got a show. This is Black girl magic." Because of a project I was doing, I sent her a note and I said she has consistently shown me how to show up and be my authentic self, how to say the stuff that nobody else is going to say, and not let the penalties deter you. When I see her in spaces speaking, it reminds me that for every space that doesn't want you coming in and being your authentic self and challenging them on their BS, there are spaces that are like, "Nah, you are exactly who I want."

Rhonda

When I came back home to Angola, a company rejected me because I was female. Another young woman I spoke to had similar experiences. I decided to speak out, and it was hard because we are told to be quiet about our plans and professional next steps. But, if I don't platform myself, how will other young women feel represented? Girls began to approach me and say, "I heard your story, and I was about to give up, but you have inspired me." I realized I was being a career advisor, even though I'm young. People sympathize with the story, not just by telling it, but by living it. I'm leading by example, showing them what they can do.

Alda

I was watching a cartoon with my niece, and it was about a bunch of different superheroes but also had a little Black girl: a superhero named Bumblebee. She was a little scientist as well, and I thought that was so adorable. She was cute and shy, and she liked her science stuff, and it was such a cute representation. All of the characters were fleshed out and I was so impressed to see strong, girly, independent-minded young women. It showed that girls can do whatever, and that was nice to see because I didn't have that.

Bola

Sadly, I don't have a female Black stem hero. The power of representation is something that has been emphasized a lot more fairly recently. I was basically making up my career as I went along. I didn't have anybody to really look up to. And everybody I saw and thought that I could be like them didn't look like me. It took my own confidence and my own tenacity to believe I could get there, regardless of my color, my background, my anything.

Busola

I had an interview with lo and behold, a Black woman. Oh my god, I got so excited. I came home and told my husband all about it like, "Can you believe this has finally happened?" I ended up with multiple job offers and this company was paying the least. But because I had the experience of this unicorn, this mythical creature, I grabbed it with both hands.

Sadiqah

I considered choosing computer science and I thought I would fail. Then, I met a female professor who I completely fell in love with. She would encourage women in her classes, and we would chat at office hours. I just thought, "This woman is very competent, and I can relate to this person." I knew she was there, and also fifteen other male professors in the department, but still, you know, she was there. And she encouraged me to switch my major, and I absolutely loved it.

Hajer

I don't even think we have a Black female professor in physics in the UK. In general, say we have around twenty-five professors in the country who are women of color, not Black, across the board. Twenty-five is like a dinner party. That is a serious issue, and it impacts everything. I think it affected my experience of not knowing who to look up to, not feeling comfortable to talk to anybody in a position of power, if I had questions, or if I needed help. The first time I had a female professor in physics was my master's research project supervisor. And she really changed everything. She was the reason I ended up applying to do a PhD. And that was just from having one woman as your supervisor. Imagine if there were more women of color and imagine if there were more Black women in the sciences in general. Firstly, it will change the demographic of what it looks like to be a person in STEM, and make it more female and Black.

Estifa'a

CHAPTER 10

WHO IS A SCIENTIST?

In 1983, David Wade Chambers created a simple experiment. He gave young children a blank sheet of paper and a box of crayons and asked them to "draw a scientist doing science things." Seems benign enough, right? This simple exercise has been repeated endlessly by educators since 1983, and it has unveiled some not-so-surprising facts about perceptions of scientific prowess.

The drawings are analyzed for seven different standard indicators: lab coats, eyeglasses, facial hair, symbols of research, symbols of knowledge, products of science, and relevant captions. It's interesting to me how male this list feels. The way a list that said oven, perfume, makeup bag, and shoes would feel female. Socialization is an interesting process. You absorb, without argument or critique, ideas about the world, and you begin to produce them like they are independent thoughts.

Results of the "Draw the Scientist" test over the years have shown:

- the proportion of drawings showing women have increased from 1 percent in the first study to about 28 percent in 2018
- more girls are drawing women
- boys are less likely to draw female scientists
- as the participants age, regardless of gender, they draw more and more men

Sadly, I wasn't able to find data segregated by gender or carried out in an African country with a predominantly Black population. I strongly suspect that the trends above were exposed there as well.

What does this say about the real world? It says young people think a scientist is "a white, middle-aged male with a lab coat, glasses, and facial hair working indoors under sometimes dangerous or secretive conditions." When children are too young to decide the direction of their lives, they are guided away from becoming scientists if they don't look like the images they draw. Even in their imaginations, little Black girls aren't scientists.

What do you picture when someone says the word scientist? Despite my own best efforts, I often picture Stephan Hawking or Sheldon Cooper. It's an instinctive response in my brain to the prompt "science." When I integrated my feminist ideologies into all aspects of my thinking, I began to picture Ada Lovelace and Rosalind Franklin.

Then, I saw *Hidden Figures.*

Now, when you say the word scientist, I immediately picture the movie poster with the women walking across the NASA emblem and Katherine Johnson receiving the Presidential Medal of Freedom from Barack Obama. The reason I thought scientists were white men, and then white women, is because I didn't know any better. I had absorbed the ideas propagated in cartoons and books and my thoughts reflected that. Now, I know better.

To read a bonus chapter filled with inspiring Black women of science, go to *theshurieffect.com* for a free download.

.

CHAPTER 11

WHAT CAN WE DO FOR YOUNG GIRLS?

Albert Einstein is arguably one of the most influential scientific thinkers in the history of mankind. He was a brilliant beyond brilliant mind who essentially dreamed up one of the pillars of modern physics. Einstein maintained correspondence with children by letter, many of which are detailed in *Dear Professor Einstein: Albert Einstein's Letters to and from Children*. One such letter was from a young South African girl named Tyfanny. In a letter dated September 19, 1946, she wrote:

"I forgot to tell you, in my last letter, that I was a girl. I mean I am a girl. I have always regretted this a great deal, but by now I have become more or less resigned to the fact. Anyway, I hate dresses and dances and all the kinds of rot girls usually like. I much prefer horses and riding. Long ago, before I wanted to become a scientist, I wanted to be a jockey and ride horses in races. But that was ages ago, now. I hope you will not think any the less of me for being a girl!"

Einstein's reply?

"I do not mind that you are a girl, but the main thing is that you yourself do not mind. There is no reason for it."

This little girl somehow understood her gender to be a great disadvantage. She also made sure to emphasize how "unfeminine" she was. Over seventy-five years later, we are teaching young girls the same thing. Society has somehow dictated that girly things have no place in scientific minds and being born a girl is a cardinal sin. The media we consume and its white, male definition of scientists has made it clear to non-white girls, specifically young Black girls, that STEM is not the place for them. We need to do better. It's a big complex question. But it's also really simple.

It's about cultivating interest and supporting success.

As a society, we need to change the way STEM is perceived. Parents, teachers, and other adults who influence young people need to stop casting it as impossibly difficult. Yes, it can be difficult, but that difficulty is not insurmountable. We need to stop making the binary distinction between cute, girly tasks and boyish, complex tasks. Learning is fun and interesting. It shouldn't be thought of as gendered with things that only boys succeed in and things that only girls succeed in. Gendered academic performance might exist in the data, but that masks a complex story, and it should not be communicated to children as some unsalable truth.

SHARE DIVERSE ROLE MODELS

Expose both girls and boys to female role models in STEM. This challenges the stereotype that women do not exist in these spaces, and it allows young Black girls to point to someone like them and decide that they belong there too. Equally, it's inspiring and empowering to young boys and non-binary folks.

EMPHASIZE HAVING A GROWTH MINDSET

Praise effort over innate ability. Encourage inquiry, questions, and mistakes. Fears about being perceived as unintelligent can encourage young Black girls to avoid academic challenges, something STEM subjects have a reputation of being. Besides this, ensure that all children are encouraged to develop the skills needed to keep STEM as accessible as possible. This is everything from letting everyone play with LEGOs and improve their spatial awareness to making science clubs inclusive and engaging for everyone.

TALK ABOUT STEREOTYPE THREAT AND CHALLENGE IT

Name the monster. When appropriate, have a dialogue about what stereotype threat is and what it results in. It seems like a complex concept but give young people some credit. If communicated well, they will be able to understand and engage with it. And naming this risk and having a dialogue about it can diminish its hold. The biases present can be pointed out and the narratives rewritten.

FIX THE LEARNING MATERIALS

Remove stereotypes and biases from textbooks, hand-outs, and instructional videos. You cannot become what you don't see. With research, you will find a rich history of women contributing to the development of not only STEM but all fields of inquiry. Where you cannot find historical role models, name the women working today. In scenarios where avatars have a gender, they should be male, female, and nonbinary without perpetuating harmful stereotypes.

PROVIDE AUTHENTIC STEM ENGAGEMENT OPPORTUNITIES

Maybe it's a field trip, maybe it's a talk at school, but provide access points that bridge academic engagement with the real world. This allows students to build up their mental pictures and create the fleshed-out dreams that can be incredibly vital sources of internal drive and motivation.

PROVIDE BETTER AND MORE INCLUSIVE CAREER ADVICE

Career counselors are an important part of the process of planning our lives and receiving encouragement and support. If you have career counselors who perpetuate stereotypical choices, this can result in stereotypical outcomes. They introduce limits on young people when they should be a gateway to multitudes.

ACTIVELY RECRUIT GIRLS INTO STEM ACTIVITIES AND PROGRAMS

A conscious effort needs to be made to get a critical mass of young girls involved in STEM-centered activities. We cannot expect diversity at later stages if the gap widens here. Fortunately, many initiatives and organizations have stepped up to the plate. Stemettes, an organization in the UK, runs various events—both online and in person—that allow young people who self-identify as female to do STEM-related group activities and meet role models. Black Girls Code in the US runs workshops, summer camps, and hackathons to empower and encourage young Black girls. Support and engage with these programs.

RECONSIDER THE WAY YOU SPEAK ABOUT GENDER

Children are perceptive. They take everything in. Please refrain from placing them into a box. Be careful and vigilant about the gender roles you imbue them with. The social script we use enforces gendered expectations that harm all of us. And these gendered expectations are one part of the gap that persists in STEM. For example, scientific inquiry requires patience, curiosity, hard work, and rebounding from mistakes. These aren't gendered skills.

The bottom line is this: it's okay if they find it difficult, it's okay if they don't choose further study or work in STEM-related fields, but it's not okay if they think it's impossible.

PART 4

TAKING UP SPACE IN FURTHER EDUCATION

I REALLY SHOULDN'T BE HERE

My life changed in a few hours.

I was in Lusaka waiting for my visa. My parents weren't in the city, so I was alone. Each morning involved a call to the embassy to ask about my visa (they often replied with some version of "We have no idea when you'll get that back, Miss. Just keep checking."), binge watching old seasons of *Keeping Up with the Kardashians* and the *Star Wars* prequels (which I only just finished watching three years later), and pacing. I am an impatient person, so each afternoon I went to the embassy, waited for their shipment of materials, and asked at the desk if my passport happened to be in the deck. One day, I decided to cut the monotony by meeting up with a friend. We were driving near the embassy, and I couldn't help myself. I asked her to drive in so I could ask, and, lo and behold, they had it. I had a travel visa for the UK. I immediately called Christina, my contact from my scholarship program, and she booked me a flight for six thirty that night. It was currently 2:35 p.m.

The rest is a dizzying frenzy. I called my aunt to ask if she could take me to the airport, got home to collect my suitcases (I had been packed for at least a week), and flew out. No long-winded goodbyes, no opportunity to see my parents or siblings, no chance to absorb the fact that I was starting a whole new chapter.

The best part of my quick departure is that I didn't have any time to be nervous. I couldn't panic about going to a new place. I couldn't worry about whether I had made the right choice. I didn't cry at the airport so I could remain emotionally detached. I had over sixteen hours of travel ahead of me, and I spent it watching endless movies. That might have been the first time I saw *Hidden Figures*. In hindsight, I think my inability to rest was its own panic.

Like most people, I had assumptions about what kind of people would be pursuing a maths degree. Movie stereotypes set out poor social skills, intense personalities, and beyond-brilliant intellect as key characteristics. Now, I am only one of these things. I was committed to approaching my transition to undergrad like a mediocre white man. I walked in, started conversations, spoke to lecturers, read ahead (though overpreparation isn't often a characteristic of mediocrity). I was excited to do well.

Then, I had my first workshop.

We were placed in groups of seven to ten to work through problems together for a couple of hours. Tutors and lecturers wandered the room to offer help or inspire a sense of panic, depending on who you asked. It was then that I met people who fit into the stereotype. One of my fellow group members was a Russian who had previously competed in Maths Olympics and another said nothing during our discussions but offered up the most elegant solutions.

I felt my blood turn cold. How was I meant to compete with these people?

I spiraled for a time. I was terrified to speak up in workshops, even when I understood the question and had vague confidence in my answer. This fear transferred to lectures and advisor meetings. I had been accepted, and I now realized it might have been a mistake. I wasn't brilliant. I couldn't do it. Passing an online test or getting a good grade on a hand-in only made me more nervous. I was a fraud who was convincingly playing my part. I thought about my departure day and how easily I shrugged off the world I belonged in, condemning myself to a four-year performance. It felt like slowly drowning, knowing it would only get harder and harder to keep up the masquerade. I would laugh to myself about the ease I felt during my sixteen hours of flight. I should have gotten a head start on worrying.

CHAPTER 12

GETTING IN

Applying to university is scary, and it can be a difficult task to accomplish. I actively avoided thinking too much about university applications. Don't get me wrong, I thought about them a lot, but I mentally framed it as a personal project to be an attractive applicant to any university. I, like most people, don't enjoy being rejected, and so I never even considered institutions like Oxford or Cambridge. Besides that, my list was based on how much I liked the city, availability of scholarships, and the standard of education I would receive.

To earn extra money, I have worked at open days at my university. Open days are opportunities to visit university campuses. I loved that job. I'm chatty and had gotten involved with different activities while studying so it was a good fit. What always surprised me was the range of questions parents and prospective students would ask me. They wanted to hear about my experiences in halls of residence, the meals I ate, the support provided by lecturers, and the inclusiveness of clubs and societies. They asked about the nightlife and the standard of coffee on campus. I wish I knew to ask those questions.

Here are questions I should have asked. How diverse is the student body? How diverse is the wider city? Do you have an adequate complaints service? Is there Black, Asian, and minority ethnic (BAME) representation in decision-making?

In 2019, an analysis of university applications in the United Kingdom estimated that Black students, on average, are 13 percent less likely to receive an offer from a Russel group university than white students (Goodkind, 2020). The Russel group is an association of publicly funded universities in the United Kingdom. It is not a British alternative to the Ivy League, and being a member of this group does not mean that you are necessarily attending one of the best universities in the country. That being said, many members of the Russel group do rank highly on league tables, and their graduates have successful employment outcomes. It is concerning to have such a large acceptance gap. Given the context provided in earlier chapters, we now have some ideas of what caused this. And knowing this fact is bound to dissuade even more Black students from applying.

One hypothesis provided for the acceptance gap is that Black students are more likely to apply to oversubscribed courses such as Law and Medicine, and the extreme competition is to blame for their lack of success. However, Boliver (2016) found that when this numerical competitiveness is accounted for, Black students are still less likely to receive offers. Another study by Parel and Ball (2013) found that when considering acceptances to Oxford, white students were up to twice as likely to receive an acceptance despite having the same grades as their ethnic minority counterparts. Of course, we can debate the veracity of this analysis. How many and what factors need to be considered to allow students to be comparable? How long of a time horizon do we need to consider? Research can be difficult to do, especially given the highly sensitive information required for such an analysis. We should work to understand this gap, but it's more important to close it.

Recall my comment about the Oxbridge universities. I, without objective evidence, self-selected to be outside of the set of people who would be successful applicants to Oxford and Cambridge. I don't really know why I decided that, but I'm sure many people can relate to vaguely understanding something to be out of reach. How many Black students are self-selecting themselves to be a part of some lesser academic group who wouldn't get into certain universities and colleges? Think about how this would impact the stats.

Let's consider the costs of applying to university. This is both economic and otherwise. Many systems involve the payment of an application fee. Besides this, it takes hours and hours to write personal statements; contact, support, and motivate references; research various institutions and degrees; and repeatedly calm yourself down. This is especially difficult for someone who might not have the network or experience to aid them in navigating such a process. Or someone who might not have too much time to spare because they have a part-time job or take on a fair amount of the responsibilities in their home. This is often true of young, Black women who are more likely to be culturally expected to play an active role in supporting their family.

Besides this, Black students and other students of color are often told they are beneficiaries of affirmative action schemes or diversity quotas. Because they obviously couldn't make it in based on their own merits, right? Affirmative action and diversity quotas can be positive, imperfect tools to improve outcomes for underrepresented groups. Sadly, they have become a beating stick used by angry and uncomfortable individuals who exist anywhere on the spectrum between actively racist and racially inept and an excuse provided by institutions when we question their lacking diversity. Meritocracy is a myth and systems must make adjustments to be fairer. Instead, Black women and other minority students feel like diversity symbols and not like intelligent students who deserve to be there and enjoy the experience. Why isn't anger and vitriol of equal intensity pointed in the direction of legacy students who get in because their parents did? Or, fraudulent recruits who come in as sports recruits á la college admissions scandal? Interestingly, white women are the greatest beneficiaries of affirmative action, not the Asian or Black students most people would assume (Massie, 2016).

Abigail Fisher took it one step further. She was the plaintiff in a Supreme Court of the United States case for discrimination (Strauss, 2012). She claimed students were selected to go the University of Texas at Austin over her because of the color of her skin. Abigail can be described as a red-haired white woman.

Now, everyone is allowed a legal recourse. But, I don't understand the basis of her case. On paper, she wasn't going to be accepted anyway. In-state applicants who are in the top 10 percent of their graduating class gain automatic admission to the University of Texas at Austin. Abigail was not in this group. She had to compete with everyone else for the remaining 841 spaces. She claimed the admissions policy, which included tests scores and socioeconomic circumstances, gave an advantage to students of color over her. Of the forty-seven slots given to students whose academic scores were worse than hers, only five were non-white. There were also 168 Black and Latino applicants with grades as good as or better than Fisher's who were rejected. The school's rejection rate that year for the remaining 841 openings was higher than the turn-down rate for students trying to get into Harvard (Hannah-Jones, 2016).

This was never a question of her individual slight but one of the validity of racially contextualized treatment. Abigail was a trojan horse. She was going to be the precedent: the case that allowed the legality of affirmative action to unravel. Wow, excuse my contempt, I just cannot understand where she got the audacity to do this. Fortunately, this case lost. Depressingly, it was not a unanimous decision.

CHAPTER 13

RACIST PLACES
AND FACES

*If you are neutral in situations of injustice, you have chosen
the side of the oppressor.*

—DESMOND TUTU

In the fall of 2013, Kimiko Matsuda-Lawrence, then a Harvard undergraduate student, began a multimedia project: "I, Too, Am Harvard" (Cort, 2015). She interviewed over forty Harvard students who identified as Black, and they shared the ugly comments and un-understandable questions their white "friends" and classmates had asked them. It is quite the greatest hits list of racist microaggressions and diminishing stereotypes about non-white intellect. Ms. Matsuda-Lawrence created a play based on her interviews, and another Harvard student, Carol Powell, created a photo project. It consists of non-white students holding up signs communicating the microaggressions thrown their way and their reactions to them. Some examples include:

- "What are you?" is not an introduction.
- No, I will not teach you how to twerk.
- "You're lucky to be Black...so easy to get into college."
- I'm "pulling the race card." You're just being racist.
- Having an opinion does not make me an "angry Black woman."
- "You're really articulate for a Black girl."
- Don't you wish you were white like the rest of us?

This project was about taking up space. It was about demanding that people realize how painful and disrespectful these statements are. It highlighted that, in 2013, Harvard had a racially bigoted present, not just past.

"I, Too, Am Harvard" spread to McGill University in Canada, and the universities of Oxford and Cambridge in the United Kingdom, as well as gained support from other US-based universities such as Yale, Duke, and the University of Pennsylvania (Butler, 2014).

This is not a Harvard problem. It is an experience shared by all non-white people navigating predominately white spaces. I think about my own experiences. I remember going to a house party and finding myself commandeered by one of the other guests. He just kept talking, and it was easier to sip on my cider and listen than attempt to excuse myself. He asked me where I was from. I told him, and his voice shot up in excitement. "I've been to Zambia before you know! Beautiful country," and I thought we were about to have a wonderful conversation. Instead, he began to muse aloud how much better the country would be if we had never ended colonial rule. Explicitly, he decided our fight for independence was a foolish act that has condemned us to failure as a nation. I stood there, numb, listening. I wanted to know his reasoning, but I was also shocked in place.

That's what can happen when people "accidentally" insult you. You freeze in place, surprised someone you were speaking to, or someone you called a friend, thinks this way and this low about you and others like you. Verbal microaggressions are terrible things with a magnitude that needs to be understood. Compared to larger, more disgusting, obviously racially motivated acts, they appear to act as racism-lite and are treated as fundamentally benign.

Fortunately, I have never heard of a blackface incident happening at my own university. The same cannot be said by everyone. In 2016, eight Black medical students at Cardiff University made a complaint (Jones, 2020). During the annual Anaphylaxis charity play, one of their white classmates impersonated the only Black lecturer as hyper-sexualized with blackface makeup and a black sex toy tied around his waist. They did this on a stage!

When the complaint was made, the university administration suspended the thirty-one students who participated in the play. They also shared the letter of complaint with them. The only Black students had a massive target drawn on their backs and lectures became daunting spaces. The university held an independent inquiry but did little to protect and support the complainants. Of course, the thirty-one students were allowed to return to school while the Black students who had made the complaint continued to feel unsafe.

A statement from Cardiff university at the time in part reads as follows: "(a) wide range of support was provided which included supporting members of the complainant group to move house, change clinical placement locations, access counseling and support [...] What the university does recognize is that it failed to foresee the depth of reaction and ill-feeling amongst the medical cohort of students and that we were unable to influence or intervene in a manner that was able to prevent the very deep hurt caused by the breakdown in friendships and peer group relationships that we know impacted so heavily on some members of the complainant group." They did not foresee that naming complainants would endanger them? That's interesting. Yet, I suspect they understood that naming the students who had done this terrible thing would negatively impact their lives going forward.

To the eight students who stood up for their rights to be respected, I commend you.

Another movement that inspires me to no end is the Rhodes Must Fall campaign. It began in Cape Town, South Africa. The University of Cape Town is ranked as the best on the continent. Once upon a time, it was my dream school: an African mecca of intellectual engagement in one of the most beautiful cities in the world. Chumani Maxwele, a South African political activist, hurled a bucket of human excrement at the statue of John Cecil Rhodes, which sits on the campus (Fairbanks,

2015). "Where are *our* heroes and ancestors?" Maxwele demanded. In my mind, that statue is a physical celebration of a man who did not see the value of Black lives, a man who pillaged the wealth of African countries, a constant reminder of the foundational philosophy of white supremacy underpinning the institution. This action was the match that ignited a national and international campaign to stop memorializing John Cecil Rhodes and the larger system of oppression he represents.

When you walk along the Royal mile in Edinburgh, you'll pass a bronze statue with a gleaming golden toe, polished clean by people rubbing it for good luck. It's a statue of David Hume, a man who once wrote, "I am apt to suspect the negroes, and in general all the other species of men... to be naturally inferior to the whites." (Hume & Haakonssen, 1994)

On June 3, 2020, five young women, whom I have immense respect for, started a petition (Akeke, 2020). They demanded that Professor Peter Mathieson, principal of the University of Edinburgh, stand with his Black students and other persons of color in the wake of the racial reckoning brought on by the deaths of George Floyd, Breonna Taylor, Ahmaud Arbery, and Belly Mujinga. An acknowledgment of the uneven impact of COVID-19 on Black and minority ethnic (BME) individuals within the United Kingdom and also internationally and a response to the racist and xenophobic actions against Asian people, specifically Chinese individuals. They asked for decency because the decent thing would be acknowledging wrong and doing your part to make it better.

I believe that the requests of the founders of the BlackEd Movement are a good example for all institutions, especially academic institutions. Their demands were as follows:

AIM 1: MAKE A STATEMENT ON THE MAIN UNIVERSITY PLATFORMS

This involves directly acknowledging the experiences of BME students and rebuking manifestations of racism.

AIM 2: PROMOTE AND ESTABLISH AN ANTI-RACIST CULTURE

Committing to an actively anti-racist culture is not simply highlighting worrying statistics but creating and, crucially, enforcing measures to prevent racism. This includes informing and educating all students, academics, and support staff on the reality and consequences of racist behavior.

AIM 3: DEVELOP A COMPREHENSIVE ZERO-TOLERANCE POLICY

A clear policy must be created with explicit penalties that make it clear that racism, discrimination, and microaggressions are unacceptable. Induction activities must include cultural sensitivity training. Signposting to other relevant resources supports the idea that this is a necessary, personal responsibility.

AIM 4: CREATE AND SUPPORT REPRESENTATION INITIATIVES

Actively work to diversify staff and students. And once this is done, create and support initiatives to serve the various demographics. Different people need different things and institutions need to be cognizant of that. A specific example highlighted is the need for race-conscious counseling services that can be provided by the university or through a recommended outside hotline.

Thank you and well done to the five women who wrote this letter and gave me an incredible example of activism and self-advocacy to look up to: Timmy Pinnick, Martine Irakoze, Mukai Chigumba, Tumi Akeke, and Dorcas Baah.

BLACK WOMEN ON UNIVERSITY

I was always very conscious of what university to apply to. I would think, are there a lot of Black people there? I would look into the African Caribbean Societies to see how active they were on campus. I went to a sixth form that was really quite white. There were fewer than ten Black people in a cohort of around three hundred. I decided I need to not be the only one in the room again.

Oyinda A.

We're training statisticians without teaching the history of statistics and how it came about. That's a disservice. We use all these methods and ideas, but at the core, they were created by eugenicists; they were white supremacists. I read the Angela Saini book *Superior* about the comeback of racial science, and it gives me pause because I've noticed that type of thinking in my own department, especially with people doing statistical genetics— the question of including or excluding race and why. I've had classmates say that they include race because there might be biological differences. We know that's not true. If there appear to be biological differences, it's because of ancestry, not race. Race is a social construct, and genetics are scientific realities. And I feel like people conflate these two very different things, and it scares me.

Jasmine

My AP chemistry teacher was white and had also worked in industry. She encouraged me, but she also put a little bit of a damper on things because she went to Virginia Polytechnic Institute, and she made me think I needed to go to that school in order to be a successful engineer, as opposed to the HSBU (historically Black college and university) that I ended up going to. It was the first time that I realized that I might have to do what is mainstream and expected by the white establishment in order to be validated. And I struggled with that my entire undergrad. No matter how high my GPA was or whether I had internships every summer, I worried I wouldn't be considered an academic.

Karrin

We went on our visit to Stanford. I thought that I would be the only Black person there, but there were two others: Emmanuel, who was an African international student, and Yukiko, who was half Japanese. We asked for our advisor and the department chair said, "Oh, it'll be Hillier. He's the person who takes care of diversity and stuff like that." "I'm sorry, did you say, 'and stuff like that'?" I was so offended. So, I put it in my evaluation because it really made me question where my place would be in the department.

Rhonda

One thing that I definitely struggled with a lot, and it did affect my mental health and my performance in some classes, was thinking of myself as a scientist. Am I really a scientist? Or was that just something that I used to say when I was younger? In my classes, I faced a lot of sexist microaggressions like being interrupted. I hate it, and I have been interrupted so many times. I would be answering a question, making my point with my laid-out train of thought. When I'm about to land my plane, Brad from the back would jump in, and I would struggle to recover my train of thought. It made me kind of anxious and self-conscious, and that really dealt a blow. If I had a male lab partner, they would take over everything and make me the errand girl. Go pick up this pipette, do this, watch that, even if I asked to help. And when it came time for lab reports, I couldn't write them because I didn't have the results. I had to lean on them to get my information for my lab report. And it made me feel even more stupid. Like, I'm not supposed to depend on you for this. This is supposed to be a partnership, and you have demoted me.

Cecirahim

At university, there was a nice mix of cultures, but you can count on your fingers how many Black students there were. How many Black females? I guess I was the only one. I decided not to see it as a limitation but as a privilege because I could never be unseen. And people got to know me, not only by my name but because I was an African. I felt like my positive reputation could break the narrative that Africans don't think.

Alda

Affinity networks, like the university's race equality network, are really beneficial to building a sense of community. It is easy to walk around campus and think you're the only one. But there are others and institutions need to support these groups, and one way to do so is by producing results in the pursuit of diversity and inclusion.

Emily

I think professors don't really put themselves in the shoes of their students, especially their minority students, especially the Black students, the Indigenous students, the Hispanic students. They don't realize what it means to be a person of color in academia, and because they don't take the time to understand, they don't know how to support us.

Malika

At university, we were all aspiring engineers. In my class of electrical and electronic engineers, there were about 106 people and only five of us were girls.

Busola

Looking at the statistics of ethnicity versus grades, there's a clear attainment gap. People of color consistently get lower grades than their white counterparts at my institution in the physics department, and I'm sure the trend follows across the board in the university. And there's a reason for that. It's because we're struggling more. We have to deal with more, and we have a harder time within the system. And so, I think at the end, even if we have a lot of Black students going into STEM subjects, how many of them are going to continue? How can they get to the top if they leave?

Estifa'a

It was very frustrating. I wanted to give up so many times and I felt so defeated my entire freshman year. In high school, I finished fourth in my class. I was an honor roll student in high school, but I was suddenly getting Cs in college. It was a huge adjustment. I remember attending a conference my freshman year for the National Society of Black Engineers and they had a career fair. I went up to one of the booths with a Black female representative. She asked for my GPA, and when I told her what it was, she handed my resume back to me. That moment scarred me for the rest of my college career. I was literally busting my butt trying to pass my computer science class and that didn't matter. How hard I was working didn't matter. The fact that my GPA was not a 3.0. I wasn't even good enough for them to collect my resume.

Angela

If repeatedly, there are no Black women who are excelling, then it tells you that whoever is watching the talent isn't doing a good job. Because it cannot be that out of a class of fifty every year, the top of the class is going to be a white male.

Salome

I think professors should take time to actually learn about their students' experiences and backgrounds to be better educators. For example, knowing that some people don't have access to certain classes in high school. We find that many Black people don't have access to advanced classes, right? So then when you teach a computer science class, you can't start from a place of assuming that everyone has taken an AP computer science class. These things won't necessarily come to your mind until you have met, perhaps, like one to five black students who have said, "Yeah, I didn't take this class in high school. So, I'm coming here with no knowledge." It's a matter of just listening to students, taking in the stories you're hearing, and implementing them into your teaching style.

Blessing

I think growing up, I always thought of MIT as a very white male-dominated science school. Then going there and actually finding that there were Black people and there was a Black community. I think that was comforting. So, when I made my decision, I knew what I was getting myself into.

Danielle

CHAPTER 14

WHAT CAN WE DO FOR BLACK WOMEN IN HIGHER EDUCATION?

So what can be done? For many people, further education is a necessary rite of passage because of the professional opportunities it opens up. It is also a romanticized and romantic time when you grow as a person in many surprising ways. The structures and administration are often imperfect, and these are a few suggestions of what they can do to make it a more inclusive space for Black women in general and Black women in STEM specifically.

ACTIVELY RECRUIT BLACK WOMEN INTO STEM MAJORS

It's pretty crazy how monumental a decision that we ask people to make at the age of seventeen can be. We don't often know or understand what is involved in certain majors and programs and may defer to advisors or lean into childhood ambitions, suggestions from elders, or fun-sounding titles. The previous section explored the barriers preventing young Black girls from engaging with STEM, so they may not be aware of its range. To remedy this, be proactive in your recruitment. Reach out to schools, community-based organizations, and other channels that will allow you to access the demographic of interest.

OFFER INTRODUCTORY COURSES IN THE FIRST YEAR

When I say introductory, I mean a true supportive introduction. I know many people who have swapped out of programs or been discouraged from exploring new interests because what was pitched as an introduction was really created for students with strong foundational understanding and a fair amount of experience. This one coding class may be a true gateway for many students and will allow you to attract and identify talent you wouldn't have otherwise.

LOOK INTO ADMISSION POLICIES

Schools often expect people to have a lot of prior experience to even apply for a certain major or course. This weeds out people who may not have had the historical support or access to earlier opportunities. Revising admission policies will make them more inclusive and promote the idea of university as a true equalizer, not as a place that perpetuates preexisting inequalities in opportunity. Offer advice about your application process. What are you looking for? Make it clear to your admissions teams that you care about the whole person, not just their grades, and be genuinely open to all kinds of people. Look at the data. Who is being left out? Make changes, scrutinize the results, and iterate.

MAKE BIAS TRAINING COMPULSORY

Borrowing from the BlackEd movement, we need to make diversity and inclusion training compulsory. This is for all academic and nonacademic staff as well as incoming students. Building on this, there should be a push to equip students in positions of power. I was required to attend sexual harassment training when I was on the committee of a student society. I should have also been expected to attend bias training so that I would be better equipped to ensure that my society was inclusive. Many people are not malicious. Awareness building is an important first step. Let us not allow people to claim they didn't know they had done something wrong because it could be at a great cost to your minority students.

UPSKILL YOUR LECTURERS

Teachers and lecturers are two different types of people. If you're lucky, your lecturer will also be a skilled teacher. University is difficult, the timelines are tight, and if your lecturer presents information in a way that assumes everyone will automatically understand it, that locks people out. This is especially true of the abstract nature of many STEM subjects. It is especially detrimental to students struggling with imposter syndrome, feeling included and deserving of their place. When the content is taught better, it becomes less a question of historical advantage or innate brilliance but one of hard work and interest, a more level playing field.

TAKE PROACTIVE STEPS TO SUPPORT THE BLACK WOMEN YOU HAVE ON CAMPUS

Host events and provide spaces where they can build a community of support. Fund these activities. Support student-run organizations that serve these groups. Provide them with an advisor who can advocate for their needs at an administrative level. Your institutions need to change and adapt to your changing demographics, and you can only do this if you listen to them. Defer to their better judgment, and do not assume you know better.

INVEST IN MENTAL HEALTH FACILITIES

This shouldn't surprise you. Colleges and universities are notoriously under-resourced when we consider mental health facilities. All of us deserve access to adequate mental health resources. Black women specifically are navigating a complex social experience. Statistics have shown Black women are more likely to experience mental health disorders such as anxiety and depression (Rethink Mental Illness). We also need to account for how existing at the intersection of race and gender and the combined effect of that may impact them. Important note: Please do recruit diverse mental health professionals. If I, as a Black woman, am working through a racist experience, I shouldn't have to do the emotional labor of providing a palatable description for a white counselor and prepare to defend myself if they choose to invalidate the reality of my experience as a result of their own blind spots.

IMPROVE DISCIPLINARY ACTIONS FOR REPORTING AND DEALING WITH COMPLAINTS

Take a stance that makes it clear you do not tolerate racist or sexist behavior be it microaggressive or more obvious and louder. Have a clear procedure for reporting and managing these issues. Have harsher and better-contextualized punishments in place. This matches the impact of the incident on the victim and dissuades people from leaning into these baser actions to gain social capital. Involve people of the relevant lived experiences in creating and updating these policies. They have a more grounded experience than others and can speak to changing trends and actions on campus.

DECOLONIZE THE CURRICULUM AND YOUR CAMPUS

Let me appeal to your ego: As institutions of enlightenment and thought creation, opening up the content you share with regards to the identity of its creator, locale, and the reality it represents enriches the academic rigor. Let me appeal to your decency: All our experiences are valid, and as the gatekeepers, it is only fair that you welcome all kinds of thinkers into the fold. Let me appeal to your senses: The world has changed. It is complex and multifaceted and deserves to be represented as such. There are assumptions and preexisting conditions, which you need to account for outside of a white, Eurocentric context. How we think about food, technology, architecture, and construction will be different in Lusaka and Washington, DC. What medical texts need to be rewritten to weed out race-based science? Acknowledge the fact that some of the greatest minds in statistics such as Sir Francis Galton, the man who discovered regression to the mean and defined the concept of standard deviation, were eugenicists. You are not preparing your students to operate in the real world if the world you teach them about is only a tiny slice of it. It also has a massive tangible, social benefit. An easy example is realizing how many lives would be saved and positively impacted once we decolonize medicine. We will lose racist ideas that claim Black people have a higher pain tolerance or thicker skin and gain an understanding of the way symptoms of disease are reflected in non-white bodies.

COLLECT DATA, SET BENCHMARKS, REVIEW, AND REPEAT

How do you know that you are making progress? You need to know where you started, where you end up, and which actions caused what. That is the only way to build a continuous loop of improvement. It holds you accountable to yourself and other stakeholders. This critical transparency drives awareness and change. Invest in collecting the data to serve the longer-term goal achievement. You do not want to be called out in ten years or five or even two having made no progress.

PART 5

BLACK GIRL SURVIVAL GUIDE

CHAPTER 15

IMPOSTER SYNDROME 101

I still have a little imposter syndrome.... It doesn't go away, that feeling that you shouldn't take me seriously. What do I know? I share that with you because we all have doubts in our abilities, about our power and what that power is.

—MICHELLE OBAMA

I am a recovering high achiever. After years of partly defining myself by my grades, I was humbled by the academic rigor of higher education. Now, university is difficult. We know this. We expect it. But it still hits you like a ton of bricks. Most people are not prepared to think and perform at university level. I remember a meme I saw online once. It compared A levels, a typical pre-university qualification in the United Kingdom and internationally, and university. A levels were like going paintballing with your friends; university is parachuting into a war zone. It's a massive jump in rigor and assessment expectations. And this often shows in a student's grades. I thought I was an intelligent person, but university made me doubt this greatly.

The term imposter syndrome was introduced in 1978 by Dr. Pauline Clance and Dr. Suzanne Imes. Unsurprisingly, this phenomenon was named in a paper titled "The Imposter Phenomenon in High Achieving Women: Dynamics and Therapeutic Intervention." They described it as an individual experience of a self-perceived intellectual fraud. Someone suffering from imposter syndrome believes they are somehow deceiving those around them into thinking they are competent. They live in constant fear of being caught.

Sitting in workshops with brilliant young people who always seemed to be seven steps ahead of me was terrifying. I never wanted to contribute, for fear of saying the dumbest, most inane thing. The two worst words on a lesson plan were "collaborative problem-solving." Every time I survived a test or assignment, I felt like I was prolonging the inevitable: the moment when they realized I was an admissions error and asked me to leave. My nerves were ragged. Studying on a full scholarship, I felt incredibly lucky, and luck became how I perceived every success. It was all down to dumb luck and once my luck ran out, I would be exposed.

I felt so lonely, but the reality is that many people around me must have been feeling the same way. It is estimated that 70 percent of people have these feelings at some point in their life (Sakulku, 2011). This can be exacerbated by environments and contexts such as starting a new job, or in my case, starting university. High-stakes changes can bring on anxiety, stress, and even depression. Think back to a situation when you were trying to prove yourself, and I'm sure you will relate to the feelings listed here.

Research has shown that imposter syndrome is felt more commonly and intensely by minorities (Cokely, 2013). Having few or no role models to look up to and emulate, as well as feeling alien to your environment, can negatively impact your confidence, especially if you are from a group stereotyped to be less competent, and aggravate feelings of imposter syndrome. This can be due to the impact of stereotype threat, which we detailed in an earlier chapter. In a harsh reaction to your minority status or even due to an unsaid expectation of the powers that be, you may have to work twice as hard to prove that you deserve to be there.

In her book *The Secret Thoughts of Successful Women,* Valerie Young described the five types of people who experience imposter feelings.

PERFECTIONISTS
People who set really high goals for themselves will feel incompetent for the slightest mistakes.

EXPERTS
People who feel like they need to know everything before beginning any project. They need to meet every criterion

before they apply for a job opening and avoid asking questions for fear of looking stupid.

NATURAL GENIUSES
Someone who is used to things coming easily to them. When they have to use effort to accomplish something, it's evidence they are not good enough.

SOLOISTS
These people need to accomplish tasks on their own. Needing help makes them feel like a failure.

SUPERWOMEN
These people work to succeed in every corner of their life. They need to be the hardest working person in the room to prove they deserve to be there.

I have been all these people. And the weight of the unsaid expectations I placed on myself was an impossible load. What causes this? There isn't a definitive answer. In my case, I would say it was an entire childhood of being defined by others as intelligent and holding on desperately to this singular definition of intelligence. If you are predisposed to anxiety or feelings of neuroticism, have high external expectations placed on you, or feel the need to compete with those around you, you are likely to fall into one or more of the categories above. Stereotypes such as "the strong Black woman" typify the superwoman type. It can help to understand what brings about these feelings for the purposes of healing. But it's okay to not know why you feel how you feel.

WHAT CAN YOU DO?

Believe me when I say you are good enough just as you are. I admire you for pursuing excellence (note that I said excellence and not perfection). Be kind to yourself while you do it.

Here are a few thoughts you have when you experience imposter syndrome:

- "I must not fail" to pressure yourself into maintaining an exceptionally high standard of work.
- "I feel like I shouldn't be here" when you feel like your surroundings are somehow above you.
- "This is all due to luck" as a way to downplay evidence of your skill.

Negative self-talk, like the examples above, will wreak havoc on your mental health. You don't have to live like this. Here are ten tips that can help alleviate your feelings of imposter syndrome:

1. Name the feeling—Awareness is the all-important first step. Call it what it is: imposter syndrome. You are not an imposter; you just feel that way. Everyone around you has probably felt the same way and the fact is, you can't all be imposters.
2. Talk about it. You will be surprised how many people around you feel the same way. One random Tuesday,

when I was exhausted from wallpapering my feelings, I broke down and opened up to a friend. He is one of those annoyingly exceptional people, and I didn't expect him to understand what I meant. But he felt the same way; he was just a little better at keeping up the charade.

3. Rewrite your mental narratives and programs. Imposter syndrome can come from seeing yourself to be inherently less than. You need to unlearn this and reframe your thoughts. Your insecurity is normal. It's normal not to know everything. It's normal to need help.

4. Appreciate the learning opportunities. You may feel like an imposter because you respect the environment you're in, the task you're doing, and the people you're doing it with. Hiccups and mistakes offer opportunities for constructive critique and growth. Allow yourself to be open to learning.

5. Be kind to yourself. Forgive yourself for being imperfect.

6. Be realistic. Is it possible that you have set an extremely high bar for yourself? That could be why you don't feel good enough. Set ambitious yet realistic goals and keep them manageable. You are constrained by time, resources, and all manner of things outside of your control. Keep those in mind when you evaluate your performance.

7. Get help. Reach out to your support systems: friends, family, and even professionals.

8. Learn to celebrate small wins and build a brag bag. It's the incremental work that will define your success, so allow yourself to celebrate those small successes.

Record them in some way so that the next time you feel doubt, you have evidence to look to and fortify your confidence.

9. Stop comparing yourself to other people. You deserve to be there. You were invited, weren't you? You are at least as good as everyone else. Do not interpret someone's external presentation of confidence as the whole truth. They might be struggling just as much, if not more than you are. And even if they're not, you are the only person whose thoughts you'll hear and whose success you'll claim. Only you know where you really are and where you're going. Set your own bar and pursue continuous improvement.

10. Realize there is no "right" way. There is no roadmap to perfection. Perfection is designed to be unattainable. Your success is good and real and should be celebrated. Validate it for yourself. Forge your own path.

AN ALTERNATIVE PERSPECTIVE

In her book, *Confessions from Your Token Black Colleague,* Talisa Lavarry offers an interesting perspective. She reflects on the imposter syndrome she felt during her career. She says it was not a lack of confidence that slowed her down but the impact of systemic racism and racial bias. Imposter syndrome is a private affliction. It, in part, can be thought of as a creation of your psyche, but that is only part of the story. It is also a creation of your context. It is a lot easier to feel like an imposter if you are the token recruit, the only one in the room, or the unicorn. Diversifying all spaces and being actively inclusive not only improves economic and societal outcomes but alleviates stress and anxiety from people who do not fit the norm, such as Black women in STEM spaces, and so it can reduce their feelings of imposter syndrome. This is everyone's responsibility.

CHAPTER 16

MANAGING YOUR MENTAL HEALTH

The year 2019 was a really hard year for me. It began exceptionally. I spent New Year's Eve in Dubai, part of a week-long family vacation. I cannot describe how beautiful the fireworks display is there. It was breathtaking. The very next day, I flew back to Edinburgh to enjoy the remaining days before the new semester began. Admittedly, it wasn't an easy trip. I loved seeing my family and enjoying the energy of the city. But I wasn't healthy. I had been carrying around a consistent sense of dread. My emotional baseline was low, and I cried every day. I couldn't tell you definitively what was wrong. Yes, I was extremely busy. This meant that I was always stressed about something and constantly tired. But, beyond that, I wasn't fully myself. I felt like I was walking in a daze, catching glimpses of my fullest most joyous self and becoming acquainted with the more subdued, pensive version of me.

By the end of January, I had totally snapped. I slept all the time. I didn't have the energy to eat or socialize. One night, I recall sleeping on the floor of my room. I had sat down to take off my shoes and couldn't be bothered to get up. This was the year I began using my quote a day journal. Looking back at those entries, I mourn for my younger self. The self-loathing is evident.

It's amazing to me now how simultaneously open and closed off I was during this time. I am known to make self-deprecating comments, so I was surely leaving bread-crumbs. In November 2018, I remember telling someone who I was close to (emphasis on the "was") that I wasn't okay, and I didn't know why but I needed them to watch out for me. I applied for university counseling services. They took three months to get back to me, and then after I spent an hour overflowing with tears and obvious red flags, told me I should look out for further email com-munication within the next three months for the option to get my four further sessions. I began taking mental health days, which were what I was calling avoiding tests and parties by staying in bed.

Finally, in late October, the storm broke. I wasn't mag-ically happy or healthy. I just realized that for a week, each morning when I looked in the mirror, I smiled. That hadn't happened that year.

There is obviously more to this story. And I'm still work-ing on myself, filling in the cracks that had made them-selves known, demanding attention. The roller coaster of navigating mental well-being and mental health can feel hopeless. Sadly, many of us are not taught how to navigate this experience. Studies have shown that Black women are the most likely to experience mental illnesses such as anxiety and depression (Rethink Mental Illness). Many studies and statistics about the mental health of Black women are easily found online. If you feel like you have the emotional capacity to do so, read them. I don't want to trigger anyone. This chapter is not about convincing you of the existence of mental health issues in the Black community or scaring you with statistics. I am not a mental health professional, but here are some useful techniques I have found through my own experiences.

ALLOW YOUR FEELINGS TO BE

It is important to give ourselves space to feel and respect our own feelings. They are valid and ultimately good. If you are angry, allow yourself to be angry. Allow sadness, pride, and joy to be felt in all of their glorious fullness. I know some of these feelings may seem futile. Being angry at a racist comment and being labeled an angry Black woman is an unfair reality. But don't deprive yourself of the pleasure and privilege of feeling. An important step in feeling your feels is deciding what you'll do about them. Anger has started many a revolution and your revolution might just be an important conversation with the person who belittled you. Your pride is demanding that you realize you're doing good and enjoy the win. Your sadness may be saying something very important about how you want to live your life. If you don't allow yourself to feel, you might be missing out on internal signals.

DO NOT BE AFRAID TO SEEK PROFESSIONAL HELP

Therapy can be seen as a bad word in our communities. I remember how hard it was to tell my mum that I was in counseling. The words formed a lump in my throat and when I finally said them, I braced myself of some abstract, undefined but definitively negative reaction. Fortunately, she told me it was okay. Did she have a perfect understanding of how and why I was there? No, but she supported me. I got lucky. I hope the people in your life support you too. Know that I respect you for seeking the help that you needed to be healthy. Maybe you'll need medical intervention. I was the worst patient. Constantly trying to wean myself off my anti-anxiety medicine because I was so ashamed of being unable to self-regulate. That was dumb. Do not be dumb like me. There is no shame in medication for mental health concerns in the very same way that there is no shame in taking vitamins or something for your diabetes. I have had incredibly useful and also incredibly useless therapy sessions. It might take time to find the right fit. If you have the flexibility, be it economic or societal, to access professional mental health support, I urge you to use it—not only in times of crisis. Check-up sessions where you talk about holistic mental well-being and can celebrate progress or make plans for the future are important too.

TAKE TIME OUT FOR YOURSELF

The world moves way too quickly. A lot of us are doing the absolute most: working full-time jobs, being full-time students, parents, caregivers, support systems, running businesses, hustling to make ends meet, pursuing our dreams, doing what we have to, and of course, that time when we lived through a global health disaster. Rest and find moments to fill your cup. As an extrovert, I am surprised by how much better I feel after a night to myself. I would set Tuesday nights aside. I knew that I had free Wednesday mornings so I would not answer non-emergent messages or go out. I bought Ben and Jerry's ice cream, did a ten-step skincare routine, and enjoyed a movie. I told people I was busy because I was. I had a standing appointment with myself. Maybe your happy refueling time is a workout or a walk, religious worship or meditation. Maybe you love reading, painting, baking, or singing. Find time to do whatever it is. You deserve to be a priority on your own list. I know it will be hard to do this. But try really hard to invest in you.

LIVE YOUR LIFE AT YOUR PACE

Do what you can manage. Stop overstretching yourself. Your contribution can be small or a genuine promise to contribute later. You can be ambitious and busy and avoid being burnt out.

YOU ARE ALLOWED TO OPT OUT

You are not a bad person for knowing your limits and respecting them. I have still never seen the footage of George Floyd being murdered. I don't need to see it to feel the pain and anguish it inspires. I opted out of what I knew I couldn't handle in order to stay sane. I am still more than able to engage with the Black Lives Matter movement without seeing the video. Figure out your hard lines, your maximum capacity, and enforce them.

IT IS OKAY NOT TO REASSURE PEOPLE WHO HURT YOU

It is not always your job to make the people around you feel better. Sometimes it is, but not always. You are deserving of receiving reassurance as well. And, if someone harms you through an active action or an unintentional occurrence, it is not your job to defend their self-image. I say it's not your job because I want to make it clear you have no responsibility to do so. You can still choose to if that's what works for you. I just want you to know you do not need to get drawn into a conversation about race relations if you do not want to. You do not need to accept half-assed apologies if they feel ingenuine. My personal rule (it's a new one) is I don't say "You're welcome" if I don't mean it and I don't say "I'm sorry" or "It's okay" without cause either. I was in the business of apologizing to people who should have been apologizing to me. I valued their comfort more than my own, and I don't want to be taken advantage of in that way anymore. I don't think it makes me a mean person. I always reassure children, and if I intentionally or unintentionally cause harm, I wholeheartedly apologize. Beyond that, I do what I can to protect my peace.

KEEP GOOD PEOPLE AROUND YOU

A support system, be it biological family or a chosen family, is vital for our survival and ability to thrive. These people will enhance your life. You will take care of each other, grow each other, and enjoy shared memories. Get rid of people who demean you, diminish you, or make you feel small (I told you I would get back to this). One good friend is invaluable. This is someone you can go to and someone you can take care of.

CHAPTER 17

A PERSONAL MANIFESTO IN TEN SUGGESTIONS

I am in the habit of collecting gems of advice. Growing up and chasing your dreams is hard and daunting work. So I ask people of all ages and experiences for advice. As I have grown older and surer of myself, I have begun to see advice as useful suggestions, not rules or gospels. The reality is that I know myself best, as you do. I know my dreams and ambitions best, especially the ones I am still too scared to say out loud. I also have the final say. As a young woman with agency, I can decide whether to do something and whether it works for me. Even good advice isn't good for everyone. That is how I will frame this chapter, as a series of suggestions. I hope some of these help you. Just remember, you have total autonomy to assemble the bouquet you need.

SUGGESTION ONE: INVEST IN UNDERSTANDING YOURSELF

You are an incredible person, a whole being filled with dreams, ambitions, anxieties, and talents. Figure yourself out. Understand who you are and who you want to be. This will be difficult. Holding a mirror to our strengths also exposes our weaknesses, and it can be hard to embrace the not-so-great parts of ourselves. You will not complete this task in a day or month or year. It is a continuous endeavor of seeing ourselves fully and watching the growth and change. It involves holding ourselves accountable when we make mistakes and actively celebrating wins. When you know yourself, you can make the best choices for you, the ones that will leave you fulfilled and align with your personal definition of success.

SUGGESTION TWO: LEARN WHO TO LISTEN TO AND HOW

A piece of advice about taking advice. Some advice is good advice, and some advice is bad. Some people have your best interests at heart, others don't. There is a lot of noise out there; which of it has value to you? As a Black girl or woman, people may have extremely high expectations of you, bounds on what you can do or places they believe you shouldn't aspire to. A simple rule of thumb is anyone who says you can't should be ignored. You can do whatever you want, with some luck, dedication, and a lot of hard work. Figure out who's in your corner. And listen to the one who tells the truth. As much as you don't want dissenters, you don't want yes men either. There is a happy balance between wishing you the best and being willing to say what you need to hear. And remember, sometimes, even these best people might not know what to say or say the wrong thing. Use your self-knowledge to discern that, and don't hold it against them.

SUGGESTION THREE: EXPLORE YOUR OPTIONS

This is a book about widening aspirations. Do remember that this advice holds for all pursuits. Try stuff out. Ask loads of questions. Meet people. Your dream job is out there. Your dream degree is out there. The pathway for you is out there. You'll never know it if you don't work to find it. Check websites and books because there are a lot of STEM organizations working to diversify the space. Get involved in their programs. Attend their events. Drive your story.

SUGGESTION FOUR: DON'T FIXATE ON THE NEGATIVE NARRATIVES

Are the experiences of Black women difficult? Yes, they are. Should that stop you? No, never let that stop you. As much as it is important to engage with and understand these issues, they shouldn't become your burden. I see why hearing about prejudiced treatment and negative experiences would be poor marketing. We discuss this in order to challenge the systems of oppression, not to cow you into avoiding these spaces altogether. This goes back to knowing yourself. What do you really want? If your picture of success is clear, pursue it hungrily and passionately. The bad will exist but savor the good. And when you're there, work to make it better.

SUGGESTION FIVE: YOU DON'T NEED TO BE BRILLIANT; YOU NEED TO BE HARDWORKING

Dreaming is the first step. Making these dreams a reality requires a lot of work. You do not need to be a prodigy to excel in STEM or anything else. Yes, natural talent is helpful and incredibly annoying when you're the one who doesn't have it. Don't dwell too much on that. You are running your own race. And, more than natural brilliance, investing the time and caring about what you do is what will carry you forward. Take the classes that you need to. STEM education at later levels assumes a strong academic foundation. Jumping into physics, for example, is not impossible but it is eased by years of practice with related problems and concepts. Beyond this, it's always good to do what you can to learn outside the classroom if that is possible for you. You could join clubs at school, sign up for summer programs, or jump onto webinars. All of this not only gives you a better foundation to use later but informs your interest and plans. Develop a growth mindset. You will fail. This is a fact. Another fact is that these failures will not define your future success unless you let them. A bad grade or having to spend significant amounts of time understanding a topic is not the bad omen you imagine it to be. Learning is a process that is labor-intensive and individual. Allow yourself to learn and allow it to take as long as it has to.

SUGGESTION SIX: PLANS CHANGE. ENJOY IT

Sometimes, it may feel like you are sitting in a runaway train, unable to stop it from rushing toward a foregone conclusion. The world isn't perfectly fair and so many of us are locked in. I'm sending you strength and I wish you the agency to change routes at any time. Dreams change too. When I was a child, I wanted to be a teacher, then a librarian, a teacher again, then a hematologist, and an actuary. I was all over the board and even as I write this, I am excited to see what the future has in store. When I speak to women who are further in their journey, many of them speak to a great varied adventure. Doors are rarely shut as tightly as we imagine them to be. Are you someone who wants to get into tech who has never coded a day in your life? That's not a problem. There are varied opportunities to learn that accommodate different starting points and availabilities. Take advantage of them. Maybe you are someone who has always had a passion for chemistry, but you don't want to be a researcher or work in the industry. Maybe you've gone as far academically as you want to. Pivot and go into journalism or business. Enjoy that adventure.

SUGGESTION SEVEN: YOU DESERVE TO BE THERE

Imposter syndrome is a heavy personal burden. I am yet to figure out how to completely wipe it out. What you do need to remember is that you are deserving. By some combination of luck, hard work, and sheer determination, you are where you are. You deserve to occupy that space. Do not let anyone whisper doubts into your ear. Ignore them and call them out. Do not let the statistics dampen your ambitions. Be the trailblazer. Do not let that voice in your head box you in. Believe in yourself.

SUGGESTION EIGHT: TAKE INSPIRATION WHEREVER YOU CAN

The reality is that as a young Black woman in STEM right now, you may not have too many people to point to as role models. Remember two things: (1) Steady change is happening every day, and (2) there is a rich history of contributors who look like you whom you simply haven't heard of yet. That being said, there are still too few. Take inspiration where you can. I love Shonda Rhimes because she knows she is a badass and proclaims it loudly. I am inspired by Michelle Obama. She has lived both an extraordinary and incredibly ordinary life and reminds us all of the value of our own stories. I love Katherine Ryan's comedy. Women are funny and can occupy space while being unabashedly female. Hillary Clinton is educated and experienced, and I look to her to remind myself that each day's work adds to a legacy. Whoever inspires you, for whatever reason, take it in.

SUGGESTION NINE: INVEST IN YOUR SHECOSYSTEM

There is a lot of beauty in female relationships. A shared understanding of the world allows you to just get each other. That being said, nonbinary pals are welcome too. Maybe your shecosystem is a study group where you can get academic support. Maybe it's a mix of people doing all kinds of things. The way I think of my own shecosystem is this: How can I build and maintain relationships with women I love and admire who push me to be my best self? Have people whose work overlaps with yours because they can provide tailored advice and support.

Have people doing totally different things because of the valuable outside perspective they provide. Have people who know you to your core so that when you drift from that, they can remind you who you are. Have cheerleaders and people who call you out for being dumb. Find these important people, allow them to support you, and lovingly support them. Relationships require work. Call your friends, invite them out, and check in with them. Be active and intentional. They deserve that, and you deserve the same. Quick side note: There is a difference between a toxic relationship and a relationship you put effort into. Sometimes, people are busy or going through something. At that point, you may be doing the majority of the emotional labor. That's being a support system. If you are always doing all the work or they say things to bring you down, please let them leave your life, or leave theirs. Friend breakups are hard, but they are necessary if the relationship makes you smaller and dimmer.

SUGGESTION TEN: YOUR MENTAL HEALTH IS INVALUABLE

Your most important resource is your mental well-being. Guard it selfishly. Your peace has no value and needs to be your top priority. Be it simply feeling low or a more serious condition such as an anxiety disorder or depression, you need to take care of that first. You cannot be your best self, you cannot fully pursue your dreams, and you cannot perform at your best if you don't take care of your mental health. What I have done to deal with my own occasionally crippling anxiety is to aggressively use self-affirmations. I have an app that gives me an affirmation to say up to twenty times a day. Before that, I spent three years, on and off, receiving help from various professionals. Journaling has helped too. Maybe you want to try meditating, exercising, or being more mindful. Take these short pauses to check in with yourself and deal with the things that come up. There is no shame in struggling with your mental health. You are being brave.

INTERLUDE:

ADVICE FROM AND FOR BLACK WOMEN

It's important to find your tribe, find your people, find your network you can grow with, even if you're not all in the same field. Have people around you who are supporting you, who are pouring into you, and you can pour into them because you can't be a one-man army and get into these spaces.

Oyinda A.

Claim your space, take up space and do not spend time apologizing for being there. Don't approach people like they did you a favor. I think about moments when someone pushed me to ask for something I deserved, make demands, and raise my voice. Those were the turning points in my career. And it is hard, right? We've been conditioned to do the exact opposite our whole lives. But that's my biggest piece of advice. First, know that you deserve to be there and that nobody did you a favor; you got there on your own. And second, make the most of that and take up as much space as possible. Basically, act like you're a white man.

Estifa'a

From my experience, I had a lot of people who tried limiting me really early on. I always knew that I wanted to go to a top school, and I wanted to study something and be successful. And people always asked, "Are you sure? Are you sure you can do that? Oh, don't apply to MIT? I wouldn't do that. Don't waste your time." Don't listen. Don't let anyone tell you no. You are literally the only person who knows your potential and how much work you're willing to put in.

Danielle

Make sure you surround yourself with people. Invest in your community, invest in your network, and surround yourself with people who can encourage you. But I'd also say, don't neglect the role of you sharing your stories and your experiences with somebody else. You know, as great as it is to have mentors, allies, and supporters, you should also invest in somebody else's journey. Who's coming up? Who's younger than you? Help them out. And be intentional about your boundaries. Boundaries are so important. The only way you can get other people to respect your boundaries is if you respect your own boundaries.

Olamide

I often tell my students that somebody who meets you on the street knows nothing about you other than how you interact with them. That's it, right? Your grades will not make you a good or bad person. How you conduct yourself when you're interacting with people makes you good.

Rhonda

To the young girl in an environment that is still suppressing her from entering into tech or has fears to enter into a space usually seen as a male playing field. The rest of the world is progressing, and I need her to understand that her skills, views, and opinions are required to shape our future. Wherever she is, whatever she is doing, if she feels like she's not able to dream or nothing feels within reach maybe because of her family, financial hindrances, the country she's in or the environment. Your dreams are valid, and perseverance is key. In 2021, nothing can stop you. Use the internet to learn new things, join tech communities, and join events if you can. It is important you understand you are capable before you start running. We do not have a female Mark Zuckerberg in tech but have amazing women doing amazing things; be in spaces that inspire you.

Mbali

Don't be afraid to use your charm. People help people they like, and it doesn't matter if you're white, yellow, black, brown, or what gender you are. If somebody likes you, they will probably want to help you. So put on the charm, and things can get easier. I'm not saying you should do anything inappropriate. I think we don't talk enough about building relationships and building a rapport. How about you try approaching someone, and just being very polite and showing you've done your research and forgetting about all these obstacles that you have? How about you pretend that doesn't exist and show that you're a reliable person, that you're smart, that you're on the ball, that you're aware of what's going on and of what's going on in the market in whatever field you're interested in. And just approach a person and demonstrate yourself as worthy of that opportunity.

Sinead

Community. I love people's stories. And your win is my win. When I see that Black women are doing really cool things, it makes my own crappy day better. Seeing the community grow drives me.

Bola

Don't let people's perception of you dictate who you become. Take up space where you don't see yourself represented. It's okay to be a trailblazer. And it's good to be comfortable being a trailblazer. You know, at first, it may be scary, it may feel uncomfortable, but the best thing is paving a way for someone else who doesn't have a way to get there.

Malika

Don't forget to network. Networking is very important, not just within your close circle or company but with wider communities. Talking to people will help you move forward and meet some incredible people doing valuable things.

Busola

The systematic racism we experience as Black people in the UK is constantly discouraging Black excellence. My advice is just to remain focused. Do not become distracted or disillusioned by everything else that is going on. Work hard. And don't be too hard on yourself. My kids say, "one, two, three, well done me," and that resonates with me so much. Take time to actually reflect on what you have done, even something small, and realize you have done something that is fantastic. Even if it's just for yourself, or your friends, or your family, appreciate yourself.

Sadiqah

Maybe this is a cynical view, but I think it is important to expect that you're gonna be in really uncomfortable situations. That doesn't justify it; it doesn't make them normal. You just have to be ready and have the guts to face that. Bring up the issues when they arise. Call people out, and don't let them ignore it. But also, don't let it bring you down.

Hajer

My big message to people is to discover what you love and do it. Have no barriers.

Salome

What you can control is your resilience when reacting to setbacks.

Ama

Not all feedback is created equal. And the further away that person is from your lived experience, the bigger the pinch, if not cup of salt, you need to add to it.

Abadesi

CONCLUSION

I launched my presale campaign for this book on Tuesday, April 6th, 2021. I remember that because it was also the day I submitted my final year maths project (and the day I started my second-round binge of *Bridgerton* season one, but I digress). It was a very big day, and I was both elated and terrified. I had been working on both projects for around seven months at that point and they had hit important milestones. They were being presented to other people for judgment and critique. Four years of study and countless late nights all compressed into fortyish pages and a lifetime of experience and four years of reflection presented as a short promotional video. With *The Shuri Effect,* I was weary of dissenters—people who actively campaigned against or loudly vilified the idea that there are gendered and race-based barriers to success and attainment. I had made a LinkedIn post with the news and was floored by the support I received. Many people were kind and excited, both for me personally and for the discussion I was platforming. Some people were not. One young man made sure to tell me what he thought. This is our conversation.

D: Hi Lauryn. I've considered preordering your book because I'd like to support another young leader, but I don't see the value in me learning about this topic.

Me: Hi D. I totally understand if you don't support the campaign. I do have to call you out for saying that you "don't see the value of learning about this topic." You are a white man and that is a significant layer of privilege regardless of your wealth and other factors. A comment like yours minimizes the value of others' experiences and that's wrong and exactly the reason why you need to read the book. Do some thinking about privilege and being actively anti-racist.

D: I believe the term "white privilege" is racist. You are attributing a negative label on me and an assumption of my character, based on an immutable characteristic.

Me: I didn't call you racist. How is white privileged a negative label? It's just a factual one. Like straight privilege and able-bodied privilege, it's a statement of societal fact. You immediately assuming that I am calling you racist might mean that you have some learning and reflection to do and that has very little to do with my statement.

D: I don't know how you have inferred that I said you called me racist. I said nothing of the sort.

Me: Okay. A good place to start might be reading the book *White Privilege* by Robin DiAngelo. I hear that it is a good one.

D: I'm in a meeting; I'd like to continue this conversation at 1:00 p.m.

Thirty minutes later

D: Thanks for your patience. To summarize my thoughts, I don't subscribe to the postmodern ideas of "white privilege" or "identity politics." I believe that linking general social issues to race is building up these divides instead of removing them. Let's take white privilege for example; your ideology is telling white people, like myself, that there is something inherently wrong with them because they are white; and in many cases that they should be ashamed of it. But where is my privilege? The most recent government report highlighted *no* instances of institutionalized racism, and we have strong discrimination laws in this country. It is wrong to characterize an individual based on their race when you know nothing about their journey or upbringing. On the other hand, to tell the BAME (Black, Asian, and minority ethnic) community that they are at a disadvantage because they are not white is more so damaging. We have equal opportunity in this country and a more empowering message is, "It doesn't matter what skin color you are, if you work hard then you can achieve what you want." I understand why you hold your beliefs and that you believe they are equipping you with the best tools to be an effective agent of change. Our common goals will be the same, but our means are very different. I'm familiar with the key data to support my conclusions from both the UK and US; while I see very little data to support the concept of white privilege or the positive effects of identity politics. If you could provide these then it would be wonderful. I am aware of my ignorance and am happy to change my mind if presented with new facts that "override" my current presumptions.

Me: White privilege is not minorities imposing guilt and shame on white people. Your apparent assumption that this shame is the point of discussions around privilege speaks to your own fear and fragility in these discussions. See white fragility above. Your advice for BAME communities implies that a meritocracy exists, and that is false. Do you believe in a patriarchy? Do you think there are systems and institutions that work against women? If so, you can extend those very thought processes to the understanding of institutional racism and white supremacy. There has been significant backlash to the report claiming no institutional racism in the UK. Give those perspectives a read. It is not a robust analysis, and it is coming from a government who has, for example, deported older generations of Black and Caribbean immigrants who were brought to the UK, they did not bring themselves, labored to build this country, and were then sent away.

D: There is not a patriarchy in the UK, which is why we have a female leader. God bless the Queen. I do not believe there is discrimination against women in the British institutions. Women exceed men in so many metrics outside of the 0.01 percent of the wealthiest people alive. Most people that die in war are men. Most people in prison are men. Most suicides are men. Women outperform men in education and work up until the age of thirty (average child-rearing age). Sorry, I didn't understand your point here or the consequent paragraph. I'd like to understand, would you mind rephrasing it please?

Me: There are more robust resources online than me. In this post-me-too, post-BLM, post-stop-Asian-hate world, you can find a lot of educational content online. Please do check that out.

D: I understand.

Evidently, this was a passionate exchange on both sides. He believes what he believes, I believe what I believe, and I choose not to continue fighting him. As I wrote this book, I kept thinking about you, the reader. How do I present the information honestly and factually? This book is, in part, auto-ethnographic; I reflect on my own experiences and present them as a part of the wider cultural, social, political, and economic landscape. Through my many interviews, I heard stories eerily similar to my own and many stories that shocked, saddened, inspired, and uplifted me. I scoured the internet for research about Black women, and it was shockingly scarce. That did not deter me from grounding my discussion in facts. Why? Because this is a mini clapback. It is a response to people like D who deny this reality. At the same time, this book is not for the active dissenters. I am not trying to convince the people who work to discredit this argument. I am writing for the Black women whose journeys we explored and for the imperfect allies who wish to know more and do things differently. We are exploring one of those complex, "unanswerable" questions. It is layered, inspires emotional reactions, and is a factual reality we need to face.

Despite what D seemed to think, I am not blaming white people or men. I am also not disempowering Black women by exploring this reality. In 1975, Toni Morrison famously said, "the very serious function of racism is distraction," and I do not disagree with her. I do, however, see great value in investing in *why* in order to understand how to move forward, for my own sake and everyone else's. It is maddening to suspect something to be true and have everyone ignore it. Researching this book was eye-opening, comforting, and saddening. The 2.9 percent figure that haunts me is rooted in so much...ignorance? Hate? A lazy preference for the status quo or the insidious impact of unconscious bias? We're at the end of the book now so I'm sure you have your own answer to the question. Or maybe, like me, that figure leads you to many more questions.

At its core, this book is about three things. Firstly, we all deserve to have every kind of dream. In this case, I am focused on the fact that young Black girls do not imagine themselves in STEM spaces, and those who imagine it get systemically pushed out. If you have vulnerable characteristics or are currently severely underrepresented, that can make it hard to dream in a way that expects success if you were to try.

Secondly, complex problems have complex and layered origins so changing them will require multiple interventions at every level. We dove into the early years and university because my lived experience allowed me to speak about those with a grounded understanding of the issues at hand. Each of these parts ended with recommendations. Those lists were not finite, and I challenge you to do more research and, more urgently, take actions in your own lives to help bridge the gap. I hope that the figure two-point-nine haunts you the way it haunts me and drives you to be a force for change.

Finally, this book exists because I wish I had read it years ago. I wish I had been warned. I wish I had been empowered. I wish I was prepared. I know that so much of life is learning by doing, but if this book had existed in 2017, I would have felt less alone, less incapable, and more seen. To all the beautiful Black girls reading this book, I see you, and I hope you saw yourself within these pages. Yes, we discussed some scary truths, but I do not mean to deter you. Change is happening every day, and while it may feel slow, I need you to be an immovable force on course to achieving your wildest dreams, whatever they may be.

INTERLUDE:

BLACK WOMEN ON BEING INSPIRED AND THE MOMENTS THEY FELL IN LOVE WITH STEM

My fascination with computers and technology started when I was like six years old. I was in a store and I saw a computer, and I probably didn't know what it was at the time, but I was so fascinated by it. Fast forward to when I was nine years old, my father purchased my first computer for me, which was a Commodore 64. And it just kind of grew from there. So, I was always the only person in my class that had a computer. My friends, in elementary school and junior high school, played games after school and I was home, playing around on my computer, teaching myself how to do things.

Angela

I had a Black teacher that taught Earth space science when I was in high school. And she was phenomenal. I ran into her four years ago, told her what I was doing, and she was so ecstatic because she was really happy to have impacted someone.

Ashley

What we need is a generation of strong women unafraid to enter and thrive in spaces regardless of the percentage of representation (gender or race). As women, we need to unapologetically own our piece of the pie. I am inspired by this generation of women who are proud, fierce, and unapologetic, taking up roles and spaces women usually shy away from. The world has fractured away from the formal and usual structure where there was a set way to succeed, meaning the room for women to succeed in tech has expanded as well. Mothers of any age, career women and young women can all find careers and hobbies in tech.

Mbali

I was bullied a lot as a kid. And I had these really wonderful science teachers, especially the one who taught me physics and biology. His lab was really peaceful because nobody went there. It was that place that I could go to and just be myself, so I spent tons of time there and the teacher and I started to become really close. He would teach me things; I'd ask questions and he would show me more things. That kind of started my love for science. I realized I was really good at this thing because I was getting good grades, so I leaned into that. I just kind of made it my strength. It was a salvation in a sense, me figuring out what I am good at and who I am.

Cecirahim

It was a ten-week experience. It was my first time really being exposed to the lab and being exposed to research. As a student, I didn't know what it meant to do a PhD, and that summer was a pivotal moment. I realized what it means to have a mentor, what it means to have a sponsor and the terms of a true mentorship relationship, where someone can guide you and tell you the truth, and that helps you figure out the next steps in your career. That experience changed the game for me.

Malika

I wanted to be an astronomer when I was a child. It was one of the first things I wanted to do, and my mum picked that up and ran with it. She really nurtured the interest. I was seven or eight and she would take me to night star shows and exhibitions. I remember a plumber working in our house telling me that I wouldn't make money or enjoy working as an astronomer and my mum got so angry at him. She said, "No, you can't tell her that. Finances do not push passion." My math teacher was incredible at school, and she was a really big reason why I ended up in STEM. Enjoying maths is the reason I ended up in physics. She really cared for her students and would teach us in her own time. I wanted to do maths courses not available at my school, and she made sure I could get online classes and she made the school pay for them. She really invested in me.

Estifa'a

The core question is how do we get more people into the pipeline? How do we inspire them, encourage them, motivate them? How do we stop telling young girls to live so that one day, they can be a great wife and a great mother, versus I see a scientist in you, I see a doctor, I see a mathematician?

Salome

I didn't really consider working in start-ups until I watched the movie *The Social Network* and realized that working in tech could actually be fun. Because up until that point, the way I thought of a career in it was helping people turn their computer on and off again or plug in a keyboard. That seemed really boring. And I certainly don't want to be in a basement coding. I didn't realize that there were so many other roles in tech, I didn't realize you could be a salesperson in tech, a marketing person tech, a content creator and a copy editor. I didn't realize that and watching *The Social Network* made me realize that tech companies need so much more than engineers, and also they can be really fun places.

Abadesi

When you come from a minority community, you often don't have access to networks and so barriers exist. If you want to be financially successful and you see the price tags that come with being a footballer, or being a basketball player, or being an actor, you recognize it as a great opportunity. And although we know that realistically, the proportion of people who make it is very small, the way in which society and social media presents it allows young people to believe that it's the way out. When they come to me and say, "Miss, I want to be a football player," I challenge them by saying, "Okay, that's fine. Well, if you love sport, what else could you be? Could you be a sports therapist or a coach? Maybe even becoming a researcher in the theory of sport. Consider the other pathways which are still connected to your passion and provide yourself with alternatives, just in case you don't make it. I'm not saying you won't, but just in case" because I want them to see the other pathways. Expectations can be so low for kids. Children say I want to be a marine biologist, for example, or I want to be a lawyer or a mechanical engineer, and career counselors will look at the lack of representation and discourage them. These microaggressions cap their dreams. I had a student come to me this week and say she wants to be a lawyer. You might even argue, "Will she ever make it?" but I'm not going to damage her dream. Instead, I gave her excitement and passion. I talked to her about law within every facet of our lives and all the options like being an in-house lawyer, a solicitor, or a barrister; entertainment law versus criminal law; conveyancing and probate; and she literally just didn't know there were that many areas of law. I was breathing life into her dream. Now, whether she ends up becoming a lawyer or not, doesn't matter to me so much. What matters is that she thought it was possible.

Aisha

I can't tell you when it first became interesting because I don't remember one specific moment. I remember building my first volcano for a science project. I remember growing plants on cotton wool in class. I remember all the dinner party examples they used to explain permutations. I have had exceptional teachers and people who could not teach at all. Tests and assignments whose difficulty made me doubt myself. I stuck with maths because it was the right kind of difficulty; hard enough to challenge me but still attainable. And as I kept going, it became almost artistic. Maths in specific and STEM in general is shockingly creative. The universal truths exist, and there are infinite ways to get there, so I stuck around to see what came next.

Lauryn

ACKNOWLEDGMENTS

First and foremost, thank you to every person who reacted with excitement when I shared the news that I was writing a book. Your positivity fortified my confidence, and you kept me going.

Thank you to my family, especially my Mum, who bought far too many copies and has always nurtured the reader and writer in me.

Thank you to all of my favorite people who keep me sane. I don't know what I'd be or do without your love and laughter in my life. I adore you all.

Thank you to all of my interviewees. Your insights were invaluable, and the book flexed and grew with each conversation. You elevated my thinking, and I hope I did you justice.

Lastly, a *massive* thank you to New Degree Press, especially Eric Koester, Diedre Hammons, and Cynthia Tucker, for supporting me and pushing me. This book would not exist without your help.

———

Thank you to the supporters in my author community. The investment you made allowed my dream to become a reality and an important issue to be discussed.

Haddy Jeng

Dorcas Baah

Alison Onyebujoh

Veronique L. Porter

Melissa Espinoza

Grace Kiruja

Kate Musama Mwale

Marina Kokkinou

Yumian Zhou

Chalwe Mwale

Esther Sakala

Michael Zimba

Joanna Lew

Jennifer Smillie

Greer Watson

Muturi Njeri

David Boyd

Julia Loecherbach

Cristina Niculcea

Mirriam Chiyaba

Mutsa Malunga

Valerie Musama Ziba

Patrycja Kupiec

Charlie Bevan

Johanna Holtan

Rares Man

Susanna Richmond

Rachel Thomas

Vishal Chalishazar

Ashley Scott

Rebecca Brouwers

Steven O'Hagan

Lynsey Aitken

Sarah Turnbull

Grace Sansom

Nick Haines

Belle Taylor

Felicia Akanbi

Kaseya Chisala

Kerstern Malama

Zoe Kelly

Serveh Sharififar

Dina Elinson

Karrin Fetlon

Anna Yang

Yeoh Yi Ling

Vesela Zarkina

Renske de Leeuw

Steven Veizi
Raluca-Ioana Vintilescu
Anna Lindahl
Cynthia Tucker
Billy Byiringiro
Alberto Chierici
Taylor Whitney Johnson
Dec McLaughlin Nutrition
Noura Elssa Chua
    Keasberry
Christa Downey
Joanie Brunner
Prince Chakanyuka
Ruth Forrester
Solomon Ngondo
Abadesi Osunsade
Cristina Garcia Ferreiro
Chenela Mwale
Muloongo Muchelemba
Hoffmann Muki
Anwulika
Chendwa Chintu
Lisa Quarshie
Finn Lindgren
Hiroki Hirayama
Gavin Brown
Kevin Olding
Mr. J. A. Julian Hall
Richard Gratwick

Georgina Lane
Musonda Mutati
Chileshe Patricia Mulenga
Tirivashe Chidzwondo
Marta Wawrzyniak
Helen Leale-Green
Kayla Mozeson
Frank Chanda
John Cornilious
Ruth Paterson
Magdalena Orlowska
Lilly Carvalho
Delaine Lorio
Hayley Forrester
Kalusambu Kasapatu
Victoria Coxen
Annika Sybrandy
Clara Musama
Ann Mwangi
Rachel Macaulay
Munshya Sakala
Matthew Roberts
Elena Soper
Dax Ko
Moira Mccumskey
N. Gerrits Gapirova
Eric Koester
Dana Casteels
Jennifer Katchmark

APPENDIX

INTRODUCTION

Education for All Global Monitoring Report, Fact Sheet (2013). Accessed 10/19/2021. *https://en.unesco.org/gem-report/girls%E2%80%99-education-%E2%80%93-facts*

National Center for Education Statistics. "Table 318.45: Number and Percentage Distribution of Science, Technology, Engineering, and Mathematics (STEM) Degrees/Certificates Conferred by Postsecondary Institutions, by Race/Ethnicity, Level of Degree/Certificate, and Sex of Student: 2008–09 through 2017–18." *Digest of Education Statistics: 2019 Tables and Figures. https://nces.ed.gov/programs/digest/d19/tables/dt19_318.45.asp?current=yes*

UN Women. "Women in Politics: 2020." Accessed October 18, 2021. *https://www.unwomen.org/en/digital-library/publications/2020/03/women-in-politics-map-2020*

CHAPTER 1: STARTING WITH WHY

Anderson, Jasmine. "Women's Unpaid Labour Is Worth £140 Billion to the UK Economy." *inews.* March 4, 2020. *https://inews.co.uk/news/women-unpaid-labor-value-uk-economy-analysis-office-national-statistics-404287*

Baron-Cohen, Simon. "They Just Can't Help It." *The Guardian.* April 17, 2003. *https://www.theguardian.com/education/2003/apr/17/research.highereducation*

Ben & Jerry's. "How Systemic Racism Infiltrates Education." Accessed 10/19/2021. *https://www.benjerry.com/whatsnew/2017/11/systemic-racism-education*

Ceci, Stephan, and Williams, Wendy M. "Why Aren't More Women in Science? Top Researchers Debate the Evidence." *American Psychological Association,* 2007.

Chang, Emily. *Brotopia: Breaking up the Boys' Club of Silicon Valley.* Portfolio, 2018.

Clarke, Edward H. *Sex in Education, or, a fair chance for the girls.* 1873.

Education Endowment Foundation. "The Attainment Gap, 2017." Accessed October 18, 2021. *https://educationendowmentfoundation.org.uk/public/files/Annual_Reports/EEF_Attainment_Gap_Report_2018.pdf*

Fine, Cordelia. "Will Working Mothers' Brains Explode? The Popular New Genre of Neurosexism." *Neuroethics* 1, (February 7, 2008): 69–72. *https://doi.org/10.1007/s12152-007-9004-2*

Kinsley, Michael. "The Myth of Meritocracy." *The Washington Post*, January 18, 1990. *https://www.washingtonpost.com/archive/opinions/1990/01/18/the-myth-of-meritocracy/ff68b614-f5bd-44e3-9c66-f1f0957a3a49/*

McKinsey. "Ten Things to Know About Gender Equality." September 21, 2020. *https://www.mckinsey.com/featured-insights/diversity-and-inclusion/ten-things-to-know-about-gender-equality#:~:text=Tackling%20the%20global%20gender%20gap%20will%20boost%20global%20GDP&text=The%20research%20found%20that%20in,added%20to%20GDP%20in%202025.*

Montacute, Rebecca, and Cullinane, Carl. "Access to Advantage: The Influence of Schools and Place on Admissions to Top Universities." *Sutton Trust.* December 2018. *https://www.suttontrust.com/wp-content/uploads/2019/12/AccesstoAdvantage-2018.pdf*

Satterthwaite, T. D. et al. "Linked Sex Differences in Cognition and Functional Connectivity in Youth." *Cerebral Cortex*, Volume 25, Issue 9, (September 2015): 2383–2394. *https://doi.org/10.1093/cercor/bhu036*

UNICEF. "Harnessing the Power of Data for Girls: Taking Stock and Looking Ahead to 2030." Accessed 10/18//2021. *https://data.unicef.org/resources/harnessing-the-power-of-data-for-girls/*

Wezerek, G, and Ghodsee, K. "Women's Unpaid Labor Is Worth $10,900,000,000,000." *The New York Times.* March 5, 2020.

https://www.nytimes.com/interactive/2020/03/04/opinion/
women-unpaid-labor.html

World Health Organization. "Africa's women in Science."
Accessed October 18, 2021. *https://www.who.int/tdr/research/*
gender/Women_overview_piece.pdf

CHAPTER 2: BELIEVING YOU CAN

Bandura, A. "Self-efficacy: Toward a Unifying Theory of
Behavioral Change." *Psychological Review, 84* (2) (1977):
191–215. *https://doi.org/10.1037/0033-295X.84.2.191*

Jackson, LaTonya R., "The Self-Efficacy Beliefs of Black Women
Leaders in Fortune 500 Companies." Theses and Disserta-
tions. 337. 2012. *http://scholarworks.uark.edu/etd/337*

INTERLUDE: THE WAY I SEE THE WORLD: A STATEMENT OF POSITIONALITY

Cooper, B. "Intersectionality." *The Oxford Hand-*
book of Feminist Theory. (August 2015). DOI: 10.1093/
oxfordhb/9780199328581.013.20

CHAPTER 3: BUILDING THE WORLD FOR THE DEFAULT WHITE MALE

Allen, G. E. "Biological Determinism." *Encyclopedia Britannica,*
September 25, 2018. *https://www.britannica.com/topic/bio-*
logical-determinism.

Blewer, A., McGovern, S., and Abella, B. "Men Are More Likely than Women to Receive CPR in Public, Study Finds." November 2017. *https://www.dbei.med.upenn.edu/research/studies/men-are-more-likely-women-receive-cpr-public-study-finds*

Bose, D., Segui-Gomez, M., and Crandall, J. R. "Vulnerability of Female Drivers Involved in Motor Vehicle Crashes: An Analysis of the US Population at Risk." *American journal of public health*, *101*(12), 2368–2373. (November 2011). *https://doi.org/10.2105/AJPH.2011.300275*

Caliskan, A., Bryson, J. and Narayanan, A. "Semantics Derived Automatically from Language Corpora Contain Human-like Biases." *Science.org*. April 14, 2017. *https://www.science.org/doi/suppl/10.1126/science.aal4230*

Cantor, M. "NASA Cancels All-Female Spacewalk, Citing Lack of Spacesuit in Right Size." *The Guardian*. March 26, 2019. *https://www.theguardian.com/science/2019/mar/25/nasa-all-female-spacewalk-canceled-women-space-suits#:~:text=1%20year%20old-,Nasa%20cancels%20all%2Dfemale%20spacewalk%2C%20citing%20lack,of%20spacesuit%20in%20right%20size&text=%E2%80%9CAnne%20trained%20in%20'M',Stephanie%20Schierholz%2C%20announced%20on%20Monday*

Elks, S. "Hey Siri, You're Sexist, Finds UN Report on Gendered Technology" *World Economic Forum*. May 19, 2019. *https://www.weforum.org/agenda/2019/05/hey-siri-youre-sexist-finds-u-n-report-on-gendered-technology*

Gaffney, A. "Are Lung Function Algorithms Perpetuating Health Disparities Experienced by Black People?" *STAT*. September 15, 2020. *https://www.statnews.com/2020/09/15/lung-function-algorithms-health-disparities-black-people/*

Gaffney, T. "A Yearslong Push to Remove Racist Bias from Kidney Testing Gains New Ground." *STAT*. July 17, 2020. *https://www.statnews.com/2020/07/17/egfr-race-kidney-test/*

Gorey, C. "High-Paying Jobs' Ads Shown Less to Women on Google, Study Finds." *Silicon Republic*. July 8, 2015. *https://www.siliconrepublic.com/careers/high-paying-jobs-ads-shown-to-women-less-google*

Green, M. J. et al. "Reviewing Whiteness: Theory, Research, and Possibilities." *South African Journal of Psychology, 37*(3), (2007): 389–419.

Gross, C. P. et al. "Racial and Ethnic Disparities in Population Level Covid-19 Mortality." (May 2020). doi: *https://doi.org/10.1101/2020.05.07.20094250*

Hoffman, K. et al. "Racial Bias in Pain Assessment." *Proceedings of the National Academy of Sciences*. April 2016, 113 (16) 4296–4301. DOI: 10.1073/pnas.1516047113.

Hutchison, J. "Culture, Communication, and an Information Age Madonna." *IEEE Professional Communication Society Newsletter. 45* (3): 1, 5–7. (May/June 2001). *http://www.lenna.org/pcs_mirror/may_june01.pdf*

Kingma, B., and van Marken Lichtenbelt, W. Energy Consumption in Buildings and Female Thermal Demand. Nature Climate Change. 5. 10.1038/nclimate2741. (2015)

Koenecke, A. et al. "Racial Disparities in Automated Speech Recognition." *Proceedings of the National Academy of Sciences.* April 2020, 117 (14) 7684–7689. DOI: 10.1073/pnas.1915768117

Linder, A., and Svedberg, W. "Occupant Safety Assessment in European Regulatory Tests: Review of Occupant Models, Gaps and Suggestions for Bridging Any Gaps." Presented at the 18th International Conference Road Safety on Five Continents (RS5C 2018), Jeju Island, South Korea, May 16–18, 2018. *http://urn.kb.se/resolve?urn=urn:nbn:se:vti:diva-12886*

Lohr, S. "Facial Recognition Is Accurate, If You're a White Guy." *The New York Times.* February 9, 2018. *https://www.nytimes.com/2018/02/09/technology/facial-recognition-race-artificial-intelligence.html*

Lynn, Richard. "Skin Color and Intelligence in African Americans." Population and Environment. 23 (4): 365–375. (March 2002). doi:10.1023/a:1014572602343

MacDonald, J. "Suzanne Vega Is the 'Mother of the MP3.'" *The Observer.* September 25, 2008. *https://observer.com/2008/09/suzanne-vega-is-the-mother-of-the-mp3/*

Metz, C. "There Is a Racial Divide in Speech-Recognition Systems, Researchers Say." *The New York Times.* March 23, 2020. *https://www.nytimes.com/2020/03/23/technology/speech-recognition-bias-apple-amazon-google.html*

Mukwende, M., Tamonv, P., and Turner M. "Mind the Gap-A HANDBOOK OF CLINICAL SIGNS IN BLACK AND BROWN SKIN." Accessed 10/23/2021. https://www.black-andbrownskin.co.uk/mindthegap

Munson, D. C., Jr. "A Note on Lena." *IEEE Transactions on Image Processing.* 5 (1): 3. Bibcode: 1996ITIP....5....3M. January 1996. *http://www.lenna.org/editor.html*

Needell, D., and Ward, R. "Stable Image Reconstruction Using Total Variation Minimization." October 29, 2018. *https://arxiv.org/pdf/1202.6429v3.pdf*

Open Education Sociology Dictionary. s.v. "Androcentrism." Accessed October 18, 2021. *https://sociologydictionary.org/androcentrism/*

Palmer, K. "Changing the Equation: Researchers Remove Race from a Calculator for Childbirth." *STAT.* June 3, 2021. *https://www.statnews.com/2021/06/03/vbac-calculator-birth-cesarean/*

Palus, S. "Science Gear Doesn't Fit Women on Earth, Either." *Slate.* March 27, 2019. *https://slate.com/technology/2019/03/nasa-spacewalk-canceled-spacesuits-gear-fieldwork.html#:~:-text=NASA%20canceled%20an%20all%2Dwomen,two%20medium%2Dsize%20suits%20available.&text=NASA%20was%20supposed%20to%20have,to%20walk%20needed%20medium%20suits.*

Public Health England. "Beyond the Data: Understanding the Impact of COVID-19 on BAME Groups." Accessed 10/10/2021.

https://assets.publishing.service.gov.uk/government/uploads/
system/uploads/attachment_data/file/892376/COVID_stake-
holder_engagement_synthesis_beyond_the_data.pdf

Rivas, M. "This 9-Year-Old Basketball Player Is Asking Steph Curry Why His Sneakers Are Only Made for Boys." *Teen Vogue.* November 29th, 2018. *https://www.teenvogue.com/story/9-year-old-basketball-player-letter-steph-curry-under-armour-boys-sizes*

Rose, H. "Cynthia Nixon Thinks Freezing Cold Aircon Is Sexist. Is She Right?" *The Times.* August 30, 2018. *https://www.thetimes.co.uk/article/cynthia-nixon-thinks-freezing-aircon-is-sexist-is-she-right-98swqmxtt*

Samuel, S. "Alexa, Are You Making Me Sexist?" *Vox.* June 12, 2019. *https://www.vox.com/future-perfect/2019/6/12/18660353/siri-alexa-sexism-voice-assistants-un-study*

Sjoding, M. "Racial Bias in Pulse Oximetry Measurement" *The New England Journal of Medicine.* 383:2477-2478. December 17, 2020. DOI: 10.1056/NEJMc2029240

TUC. "Personal Protective Equipment and Women." Accessed 10/10/2021. *https://www.tuc.org.uk/sites/default/files/PPEandwomenguidance.pdf*

Weaver, J. "Design Has an Empathy Problem: White Men Can't Design for Everyone." *UX Collective.* June 15, 2020. *https://uxdesign.cc/design-has-an-empathy-problem-white-men-cant-design-for-everyone-4eef12f0f2bc*

Wheaton, O. "Gym's Computer Assumed This Woman Was a Man Because She Is a Doctor." *Metro*. March 18, 2015. *https://metro.co.uk/2015/03/18/gyms-computer-assumed-this-woman-was-a-man-because-she-is-a-doctor-5110391/*

CHAPTER 4: AFRICAN WOMANHOOD

Bordo, S "Unbearable Weight: Feminism, Western Culture and the Body." Berkeley, CA, University of California Press. (1993)

Eagly, A. H., and Mladinic, A. "Are People Prejudiced against Women? Some Answers from Research on Attitudes, Gender Stereotypes, and Judgments of Competence." *European Review of Social Psychology*. 5: 1–35. (1994). doi:10.1080/14792779543000002.

Emma. "Benevolent Sexism: A Feminist Comic Explains How It Holds Women Back." *The Guardian*. August 13, 2020. *https://www.theguardian.com/books/2020/aug/13/benevolent-sexism-a-feminist-comic-explains-how-it-holds-women-back#_=_*

Glick, P., and Fiske, S. "Hostile and Benevolent Sexism: Measuring Ambivalent Sexist Attitudes toward Women." March 1. 1997. *https://doi.org/10.1111/j.1471-6402.1997.tb00104.x*

Hochschild, A., Machung, A. "The Second Shift: Working Parents and the Revolution at Home." New York, NY: Viking. 1989.

Inter Parliamentary Union. "Women in National Parliaments." Accessed 10/16/2021. *http://archive.ipu.org/wmn-e/classif.htm*

LSE. "Africa at Work for Women." March 16, 2018. *https://blogs. lse.ac.uk/africaatlse/2018/05/16/africa-at-work-for-women/#:~:text=Employment%20for%20women%20in%20African,not%20always%20work%20for%20all.*

Maathai, M. W. *Unbowed*. New York: Anchor Books, 2007.

McKinsey. "Women Matter Africa." August 2016. *https:// www.mckinsey.com/~/media/McKinsey/Featured%20 Insights/Women%20matter/Women%20matter%20Africa/ Women%20Matter%20Africa%20August%202016.ashx*

Oyaro, K. "More Women in Politics." *Africa Renewal*. August-November 2017. *https://www.un.org/africarenewal/magazine/ august-november-2017/more-women-politics*

Tajfel, H., and Turner, J. "An Integrative Theory of Intergroup Conflict." Ark. 1986. *http://ark143.org/wordpress2/wp-content/uploads/2013/05/Tajfel-Turner-1979-An-Integrative-Theory-of-Intergroup-Conflict.pdf*

UN Women. "Women in Politics: 2020." Accessed 10/10/2021. *https://www.unwomen.org/-/media/headquarters/attachments/sections/library/publications/2020/women-in-politics-map-2020-en.pdf?la=en&vs=827*

CHAPTER 5: ACCESS GAPS

Afrobarometer. "PP61: Gains and Gaps: Perceptions and Experiences of Gender in Africa" 2019. Accessed 10/15/2021. *https:// afrobarometer.org/publications/pp61-gains-and-gaps-perceptions-and-experiences-gender-africa*

Barro, R. "Economic Growth in a Cross Section of Countries." *The Quarterly Journal of Economics*, Volume 106, Issue 2 (May 1991): 407–443, *https://doi.org/10.2307/2937943*

Bashir, S. et al. "Facing Forward: Schooling for Learning in Africa." *World Bank*. 2018. Accessed 01/10/2021. *https://open-knowledge.worldbank.org/handle/10986/29377*

Brookings. "Too Little Access, Not Enough Learning: Africa's Twin Deficit in Education." January 16, 2013. *https://www.brookings.edu/opinions/too-little-access-not-enough-learning-africas-twin-deficit-in-education/*

Darvas, P. et al. "Sharing Higher Education's Promise Beyond the Few in Sub-Saharan Africa" *World Bank Group* (2017). *https://openknowledge.worldbank.org/bitstream/han-dle/10986/27617/9781464810503.pdf?sequence=2&isAl-lowed=y*

Fox, L., and Thomas, A. "Africa's Got Work to Do: A Diagnostic of Youth Employment Challenges in Sub-Saharan Africa," *Journal of African Economies*, Volume 25, Issue suppl_1, (March 2016): i16–i36. *https://doi.org/10.1093/jae/ejv026*

Glewwe, P., Maïga, E., and Zheng, H. "The Contribution of Education to Economic Growth: A Review of the Evidence, with Special Attention and an Application to Sub-Saharan Africa." *World Development,* July 2014. *https://doi.org/10.1016/j.world-dev.2014.01.021*

Griffin, A. M. "Educational Pathways in East Africa: Scaling a Difficult Terrain." Kampala: Association for the Advancement of Higher Education and Development (AHEAD). 2007.

Habitat for Humanity. "Poverty and Education in East Africa: Breaking the cycle." Accessed 10/13/2021. *https://www.habitatforhumanity.org.uk/blog/2017/04/poverty-and-education-east-africa/*

Hanushek, E. A., and Ludger W. "The Role of Cognitive Skills in Economic Development." *Journal of Economic Literature*, 46 (3): 607-68, September 2008. DOI: 10.1257/jel.46.3.607

Human Rights Watch. "Leave No Girl Behind in Africa." June 14, 2018. *https://www.hrw.org/report/2018/06/14/leave-no-girl-behind-africa/discrimination-education-against-pregnant-girls-and*

iMlango. "Our Story." Accessed 10/11/2021. *https://www.imlango.com/our-story*

Krueger, B., and Lindahl, M. "Education for Growth: Why and for Whom?" *Journal of Economic Literature*, 39 (4): 1101–1136. December 2001. DOI: 10.1257/jel.39.4.1101

Masau, Z. "Africa Grapples with Huge Disparities in Education." *Africa Renewal.* December 2017–March 2018. *https://www.un.org/africarenewal/magazine/december-2017-march-2018/africa-grapples-huge-disparities-education*

The Education Center. "UNICEF Global Databases Based on Multiple Indicator Cluster Surveys, Demographic and Health

Surveys and Other National Household Surveys." Accessed October 30, 2020.

UNESCO Institute for Statistics (UIS). "Leaving No One Behind: How Far on the Way to Universal Primary and Secondary Education?" 2016. *https://en.unesco.org/gem-report/leaving-no-one-behind-how-far-way-universal-primary-and-secondary-education*

CHAPTER 6: AN INTRODUCTION TO THE MICROAGGRESSION

Limbong, A. "Microaggressions Are a Big Deal: How to Talk Them Out and When to Walk Away." *NPR*. June 9, 2020. *https://www.npr.org/2020/06/08/872371063/microaggressions-are-a-big-deal-how-to-talk-them-out-and-when-to-walk-away?t=1632772054080*

Sue, D. W., and Spanierman, L. *Microaggressions in Everyday Life: Race, Gender, and Sexual Orientation.* Hoboken, NJ: Wiley, 2010.

Washington, F., Birch, H., and Roberts, M. "When and How to Respond to Microaggressions" *Harvard Business Review.* July 3, 2020. *https://hbr.org/2020/07/when-and-how-to-respond-to-microaggressions*

CHAPTER 7: A NOTE TO ALLIES

Black, Asian & Minority Ethic Educators. Advice for an Ally. *https://www.bameednetwork.com/wp-content/uploads/2019/07/advice-5c-20for_38970569.pdf*

Melaku, T., Beeman, A., Smith, D., and Johnson W. "Be a Better Ally." *HBR*. December 2020. *https://hbr.org/2020/11/be-a-better-ally*

CHAPTER 8: TEACHERS, ANXIETY TRANSFER, AND STEREOTYPE THREAT

Beilcok, S., Gunderson, E., Ramirez, G., and Levine, S. "Female Teachers' Math Anxiety Affects Girls' Math Achievement." *Proceedings of the National Academy of Sciences*, 107 (5) (2010): 1860-1863. DOI: 10.1073/pnas.0910967107

Beilock, S. L., Rydell, R. J., and McConnell, A. R. (2007). "Stereotype Threat and Working Memory: Mechanisms, Alleviation, and Spillover." *Journal of Experimental Psychology: General, 136* (2) (2007): 256–276. *https://doi.org/10.1037/0096-3445.136.2.256*

Lavy, V., and Sand, E. "On the Origins of Gender Human Capital Gaps: Short and Long Term Consequences of Teachers' Stereotypical Biases." National Bureau of Economic Research. January 2015. *http://www.nber.org/papers/w20909*

Perry D-G, and Bussey K. "The Social Learning Theory of Sex Differences: Imitation Is Alive and Well." J Pers Soc Psychol 37:1699–1712. 1979

Spencer, S., Steele, C., and Quinn, D. "Stereotype Threat and Women's Math Performance." *Journal of Experimental Social Psychology.* Vol. 35, Issue 1, January 1999, 4-28

Steele, C. M. "A Threat in the Air: How Stereotypes Shape Intellectual Identity and Performance." *American Psychologist,* 52(6), 613–629, 1997. doi:10.1037/0003-066X.52.6.613

Steele, C. M., and Aronson, J. "Stereotype Threat and the Intellectual Test Performance of African Americans." *Journal of Personality and Social Psychology, 69(5), 797–811. 1995. http:// dx.doi.org/10.1037/0022-3514.69.5.797*

Van Mier, H. I. et al. "Gender Differences Regarding the Impact of Math Anxiety on Arithmetic Performance in Second and Fourth Graders." *Frontiers in Psychology*, Vol. 9. January 18, 2019. DOI: 10.3389/fpsyg.2018.02690

Zhang, S, Schmader, T., and Hall, W. "L'eggo My Ego: Reducing the Gender Gap in Math by Unlinking the Self from Performance," *Self and Identity*, 12:4, 400–412, May 17, 2012. DOI: 10.1080/15298868.2012.687012

CHAPTER 9: THE SCULLY EFFECT AND THE IMPACT OF ROLE MODELS IN MEDIA

21st Century Fox, The Geena Davis Institute on Gender in Media, and J. Walter Thompson Intelligence. "The Scully Effect: I Want to Believe...in STEM." Accessed 10/10/2021. *https://seejane.org/wp-content/uploads/x-files-scully-effect-report-geena-davis-institute.pdf*

BlackDoctor.org. "Dr. Myiesha Taylor: The Real-Life Inspiration behind Doc McStuffins." Accessed October 18, 2021. *https:// blackdoctor.org/dr-myiesha-taylor-turning-tragedy-into-inspiration-for-millions/*

Lee, Sonia. "The Image of the Woman in the African Folk-tale from the Sub-Saharan Francophone Area." *Yale French Studies*, no. 53 (1976): 19–28. Accessed July 7, 2021. doi:10.2307/2929648.

Riley, E. "Role Models in Movies: The Impact of Queen of Katwe on Students' Educational Attainment." Emma Riley. December 19, 2019. https://emmaalriley.files.wordpress. com/2020/02/role_models_in_movies.pdf

CHAPTER 10: WHO IS A SCIENTIST?

Chambers, D. "Stereotypic Images of the Scientist: The Draw-a-Scientist Test." *Science Education Assessment Instruction.* April 1983. *https://doi.org/10.1002/sce.3730670213*

Yong, E. "What We Learn From 50 Years of Kids Drawing Scientists." *The Atlantic.* March 20, 2018. https://www. theatlantic.com/science/archive/2018/03/what-we-learn-from-50-years-of-asking-children-to-draw-scientists/556025/

CHAPTER 11: WHAT CAN WE DO FOR YOUNG GIRLS?

Einstein A., and Calaprice, A. *Dear Professor Einstein: Albert Einstein's Letters to and from Children.* Amherst, N.Y. Prometheus Books, 2002.

Hill, C., and Corbett, C. *Solving the Equation: The Variables for Women's Success in Engineering and Computing.* Washington: *AAUW,* 2015.

Hill, C., Corbett, C., and Rose, A. *Why So Few? Women in Science, Technology, Engineering and Mathematics*. Washington: AAUW, 2020.

UNESCO. "Cracking the Code: Girls' and Women's Education in Science, Technology, Engineering and Mathematics." 2017. *https://unesdoc.unesco.org/ark:/48223/pf0000253479*

CHAPTER 12: GETTING IN

Boliver, V. "Exploring Ethnic Inequalities in Admission to Russell Group Universities." *Sociology 50*, no. 2 (2016): 247–66. April 2016. *https://www.jstor.org/stable/26556428*.

Goodkind, S. "Applying to Uni Is Different If You're Black: Why Unis Offer Far Fewer Places to Black Students." *The Tab*. Accessed 01/10/2021. *https://thetab.com/uk/2020/07/01/applying-to-uni-is-different-if-youre-black-why-unis-offer-far-fewer-places-to-black-students-163683*

Hannah-Jones, N. "What Abigail Fischer's Affirmative Action Case Was Really About." *Propublica*. June 23, 2016. *https://www.propublica.org/article/a-colorblind-constitution-what-abigail-fishers-affirmative-action-case-is-r*

Massie, V. "White Women Benefit Most from Affirmative Action—and Are among Its Fiercest Opponents." *Vox*. June 23, 2016. *https://www.vox.com/2016/5/25/11682950/fisher-supreme-court-white-women-affirmative-action*

Parel, K., and Ball, J. "Oxford University Accused of Bias against Ethnic Minority Applicants." *The Guardian*. February 26,

2013. *https://www.theguardian.com/education/2013/feb/26/ oxford-university-ethnic-minority-applicants*

Strauss, V. "Who Is Abigail Noel Fischer?" *The Washington Post.* October 10, 2012. *https://www.washingtonpost.com/news/ answer-sheet/wp/2012/10/10/who-is-abigail-noel-fisher/*

CHAPTER 13: RACIST PLACES AND FACES

Akeke, T. "University of Edinburgh Stand Against Racism." *Change.org.* Accessed 10/09/2021. *https://www.change. org/p/university-of-edinburgh-s-actions-against-racism?utm_ content=cl_sharecopy_22581575_en-GB%3A8&recruit- er=537433559&recruited_by_id=b07fa730-130c-11e6-bdbf- 331bb2073838&utm_source=share_petition&utm_medium=co- pylink&utm_campaign=psf_combo_share_initial&use_react=- false*

Bih. "What You're Really Saying When You Call Black Women Undesirable." Medium. Accessed 05/25/2021. *https://medium. com/age-of-awareness/what-youre-really-saying-when-you- call-black-women-undesirable-bdcfc94f5c51*

Butler, B. "'I, Too, Am Harvard': Black Students Show They Belong." *The Washington Post.* March 5, 2014. *https://www. washingtonpost.com/blogs/she-the-people/wp/2014/03/05/i- too-am-harvard-black-students-show-they-belong/*

Cort, B. "Kimiko M. Matsuda-Lawrence." *The Harvard Crim- son.* December 10, 2015. *https://www.thecrimson.com/arti- cle/2015/12/10/kimiko-matsuda-lawrence/*

Fairbanks, E. "The Birth of Rhodes Must Fall." *The Guardian.* November 18, 2015. *https://www.theguardian.com/news/2015/nov/18/why-south-african-students-have-turned-on-their-parents-generation*

Hume, D. "Of National Characters." In K. Haakonssen (Ed.), Hume: Political Essays (Cambridge Texts in the History of Political Thought, pp. 78–92). Cambridge: Cambridge University Press. 1994. doi:10.1017/CBO9781139170765.018

I, too, am Harvard. Accessed 10/10/2021. *https://itooamharvard.tumblr.com/*

Long, J., and Soen, H. "'She's a Big Black Ape': Boys Insult BU Fresher in Racist Group Chat." *The Tab.* Accessed 03/10/2021. *https://thetab.com/uk/bournemouth/2017/11/15/shes-a-big-black-ape-boys-insult-bu-fresher-in-racist-group-chat-6030*

Robnett, B., and Feliciano, C. "Patterns of Racial-Ethnic Exclusion by Internet Daters." *Social Forces*, Volume 89, Issue 3, March 2011, 807–828. *https://doi.org/10.1093/sf/89.3.807*

Silverstone, T., and Sewell, S. "'People Don't Even Look at Me': Eight Black Women Discuss Politics of Light and Dark Skin." [video]. *The Guardian.* April 8, 2019. *https://www.theguardian.com/us-news/video/2019/apr/08/people-dont-even-look-at-me-eight-black-women-discuss-politics-of-light-and-dark-skin-video*

CHAPTER 14: WHAT CAN WE DO FOR BLACK WOMEN IN HIGHER EDUCATION?

Hill, C., and Corbett, C. *Solving the Equation: The Variables for Women's Success in Engineering and Computing.* Washington: AAUW. 2015.

Hill, C., Corbett, C., and Rose, A. *Why So Few? Women in Science, Technology, Engineering and Mathematics.* Washington: AAUW, 2020.

Rethink Mental Illness. "Black, Asian and Minority Ethnic (BAME) mental health." Accessed 10/10/2021. *https://www.rethink.org/advice-and-information/living-with-mental-illness/wellbeing-physical-health/black-asian-and-minority-ethnic-mental-health/*

CHAPTER 15: IMPOSTER SYNDROME 101

Abrams, A. "Yes, Imposter Syndrome Is Real. Here's How to Deal with It." *Time.* June 20, 2018. *https://time.com/5312483/how-to-deal-with-impostor-syndrome/*

Clance, P.R., and Imes, S.A. "The Imposter Phenomenon in High Achieving Women: Dynamics and Therepeutic Interventions." *Psychotherapy: Theory Research and Practice*, 15, 241–247. 1978.

Cokely, K., McClain, S., Enciso, A., and Martinez, M. "An Examination of the Impact of Minority Status Stress and Imposter Feelings on the Mental Health of Diverse Ethnic Minority College Students." *Journal of Multicultural Coun-*

seling and Development. Vol 41, Issue 2. April 8, 2013. https://doi.org/10.1002/j.2161-1912.2013.00029.x

Lavarry, T. *Confessions from Your Token Black Colleague: True Stories & Candid Conversations about Equity and Inclusion in the Workplace.* Yum Yum Morale LLC Publishing House, 2020.

Maryville University. "You Belong in the Room—Exploring Imposter Syndrome from a Black Perspective." Accessed 10/12/2021. *https://online.maryville.edu/blog/impostor-syndrome-black-perspective/#:~:text=Why%20Impostor%20Syndrome%20Is%20More,Black%2C%E2%80%9D%20author%20Jolie%20A.*

Sakulku, J. "The Impostor Phenomenon." *The Journal of Behavioral Science,* 6(1), 75-97. 2011. *https://doi.org/10.14456/ijbs.2011.6*

Young, V. *The Secret Thoughts of Successful Women: Why Capable People Suffer from Imposter Syndrome and How to Thrive in Spite of It.* Crown Publishing, 2011.